ACKNOWLEDGEMENTS

I'd like to say a big thanks to my family for their wholehearted support and encouragement, but as I received neither of these, I'd just like to thank Maria my wife, my son Paul , daughter Stacey, Mum and brother David and sister Marie and their families for being who they are. Very much the rock on which my life is built around.

To my dad for being the man he was and introducing me to this great game.

All the events in the book actually happened (as I remember them) and all the characters are real. Thanks to all of these people and to all who I've played golf with but with special thanks to John Hamilton for all the reasons mentioned in the book.

And last but not least, to Milngavie pro David Muir, whose suggestion it was that I should write this book. For that and his help and encouragement a very big thanks indeed.

INTRODUCTION

Jack Nicklaus, Seve Ballesteros, Tiger Woods, Rory McIlroy, Brian Mooney. All of them golfing legends . Except for Brian Mooney, who's not. But for every Tiger or Rory there's a million Brians, guys who love the game and would have been legends had they only had the talent, ability and dedication required.

This is not the story of pro golf, of long raking drives, majestic towering irons and success and triumph.

This is a tale of laughter, frustration, dreams, frustration, enjoyment, frustration, hope and more frustration.

This is Brian's story.

And it's probably your story too.

FOREWORD

It is customary for a golf book to have a golfing luminary heap praise on the author and his abilities. I must confess that my golfing acquaintances cannot really count themselves to be among the golfing greats, although Sir Nick Faldo will possibly recall the time we shared a joke at the Open at Muirfield in 1980. It was on a practice day, late in the evening and Nick was on the practice putting green. Due to the lateness of the hour there was only a small gallery, and Nick threw down half a dozen balls about ten feet from a hole and methodically went through his routine. One by one the balls shaved the hole and as Nick went to retrieve them he became aware of the small band of fans, most armed with programmes or hats. He came over and started to sign his name on each with a grateful thanks from the assembled few. As he arrived at the end of the line, I stood, programme in hand at my side. He looked at me and I looked at him, and realising that there was no further requirements for a signature, he returned to his putting practice, where he holed the first ten footer he faced. "<u>Now</u> can I have your autograph ?" I asked politely.

"Eh ?" he said somewhat puzzled, either not getting the joke or not understanding the broad Scottish accent. Or…maybe he did get the joke but thought "what a tosser" or words to that effect.

So for a celebrity endorsement, what about these comments from Sky Sports commentators and golfing greats –

Rob Lee "Stellar!"

Butch Harmon "Atta boy !"

Colin Montgomerie "when I was Ryder Cup Captain…."

Now none of these guys have actually read the book, but if they did, I think there's a reasonable chance that's what they would have said.

Enjoy the read.

Contents

Chapter 1 – Getting to the Tee
Chapter 2 – The First
Chapter 3 – Lethamhill – the Glory Years
Chapter 4 – Lethamhill – the Lean Years
Chapter 5 – Crow Wood Private Members Club
Chapter 6 – Milngavie Golf Club – The First Eighteen
Chapter 7 – The Committee Years
Chapter 8 – The Open
Chapter 9 – Away Days
Chapter 10 – The Tools of the Trade
Chapter 11 – Would You Believe It ?
Chapter 12 – Home On the Range
Chapter 13 – The Milngavie Players
Chapter 14 – Not Quite Bruce
Chapter 15 – Mano a Mano
Chapter 16 – The Best of the Best
Chapter 17 – The Back Nine
Chapter 18 - Hame
19th Hole

Chapter 1

Getting to the Tee

My golfing career actually started in a classroom full of noisy weans in primary 3 at St.Modan's Primary School ("education for the intellectually challenged") in Cranhill in Glasgow's East End. It was a normal classroom and the class consisted of thirty typical kids of around seven years of age, from the genius who could recite the two times table from two times one right up to two times twelve, to the less gifted, who , when asked to paint an animal during art , pulled down his zip, took out his wee willie and painted it green and black. When questioned, he explained it was a snake, which is an animal, and you told us to paint an animal, so there it is. Which , to be fair to him, did show a reasonable degree of imagination in a strange kind of way. As an aside, I'm sure I saw the pet hamster in the cage at the back of the class breathe a sigh of relief that he himself wasn't daubed with paint when the teacher asked her pupils to "paint an animal". It was in this class and during one of my more attentive moments that my defining moment in golf came. I was looking intently at the teacher who was writing on the blackboard , when she turned round , and being pleased that one of her pupils was actually taking an interest , asked me to read what she had just written. Being one of the clever students in the class (everything is relative I suppose) I confidently answered "c – a – t ....cat." "Interesting" she replied, "when you go home tonight, get your mum to take you to the opticians." My blank look must have come as no surprise to her, having seen it on many occasions previously . "Ask your mum to get someone to check your eyesight," she said, slightly louder and more slowly than she needed to. " Come here". As I got up out of my seat and approached the teacher I noted that the c – a – t previously written on the blackboard had mysteriously changed into 6 – 0 – 7. Being quick of wit, I instinctively knew she hadn't miraculously changed it without me knowing, and I realised that I had a problem here.

So how was that the start of a golfing career lasting 45 years (and still counting) ? Well, I was duly despatched to the optician the following week and he confirmed that my eyesight was indeed getting poorer and that I needed glasses to correct the onset of short sightedness. This was a devastating blow to a seven year old kid growing up in Cranhill. Not just because I knew I was destined to be called "specky" and picked on endlessly for the rest of my life, but more crushing than that, my football career had just been placed in jeopardy. Like most boys growing up in the East End, football was my absolute passion. We would play it night and day, day and night, 5 a side, 10 a side, 20 a side, "ten – twenty wanners" (first to 10 goals meant half time, 21 goals full time and the ultimate winner). We would play on the street, in the waste land at the garages in Longstone Road or if we were daring, on the grassy land of the nursery school in Newhaven Road , where we would play for half an hour until the janny finished his can of Carlsberg and chased us off his patch. Despite being a small boy for my age I had a fair bit of skill and vision (how ironic given my eyesight problem) and was a good passer of the ball. I also had a real talent for dribbling – you could say a bit like Jimmy Johnstone of the Celtic of that era, or Lionel Messi of modern times . Friends of mine of that vintage may dispute that assertion and allude to the fact that I was more like Jimmy Krankie of the Krankies, or more Lionel Blair than Lionel Messi. However I would contend that football is all about opinions, and as an unbiased judgement, mine would surely have been closer to the mark. On the fateful day when the optician delivered his verdict on my failing eyesight, the news that I had to wear spectacles, was in local parlance , a bit of a pisser , as the teacher who ran the school team would surely not entertain the notion of me playing for the school team wearing my "Gregory Peck's". There was nothing else for it. I would wear my glasses sparingly in the classroom only, and play on without them on the park. This indeed worked for a time and I continued to play organised football, but by the time I had reached ten , the game was up. My eyesight had continued to deteriorate and unless we were playing football in the gym where the ball was never more than seven yards away, I was struggling badly. At that age, most boys flock towards the ball; instead I was running towards the flock of players, trying to suss out the ball's whereabouts….. a bit like the weakest seagull at the edge of the flock trying to see where the fish was, and by the time it gets through the crowd, the fish , or in my case the ball, had gone, and the flock had moved on. (I wish I had patented these thoughts – I could've sued Eric Cantona for plagiarism some thirty years later).

Eventually I knew the game was up, the last straw coming when I ran into a goal post, though I still maintain to this day that was due to a lack of concentration rather than a lack of eyesight.

And thus, my football career was at a premature end. Yes, I could still play football in the street, but for me, the (competitive) game was indeed abogey. My dad, who had been an excellent footballer in his day, understood and sympathised. And whilst he could do nothing to help my footballing tragedy, as a "pick me up" he suggested that he would take me and my elder brother David to play golf. This suggestion was met with absolute indifference from us both. Me, because I was still pining for the football field, David as he was some kind of weirdo. To explain, David was some four years older than me but for some inexplicable reason didn't actually play football. Instead he preferred to go fishing at Hogganfield (Huggy) Loch, which was some three miles away from our house, and listen to some kind of wailing (he called it music) from bands like Hawkwind and Whitesnake. He could also, I imagine, be found contemplating suicide in the solitude of his own room whilst listening to the songs of Leonard Cohen. Nonetheless, both he and I were persuaded that it would be worth a try, and our first golfing venture would be that very next Saturday. The venue was that golfing mecca in the East End of Glasgow, the nine hole council owned course Alexandra Park, or Ally Park as it is more commonly known. A course , which it was rumoured, narrowly missed out on being on the Open rota alongside St.Andrew's, Muirfield, Carnoustie and the rest. Some may have pointed to its lack of length and difficulty, being only some 2,000 yards long and a par 31 as being the rationale for its omission. Others have suggested the small clubhouse may not have been able to accommodate the amount of media presence that follows modern events. Perhaps the real reason for its cruel denial to its rightful place in Open history was due to the amount of glue sniffers roaming the fairways. I must confess to being uncertain on this point . I am not party to the R&A's decision making process, so the reason , to this day, remains a mystery. What I do know however, that it was, and still is , a good and fitting place to learn to play golf.

Chapter 2

The First

There is one thing that you should know about my dad. He was just an out and out great guy. I have never to this day heard anyone ever saying a bad word about him. His motto was "no problem", a eulogy that we latterly put on his headstone. He was a plumber to trade (apparently the best there ever was, according those in the know i.e. him) and a handyman with a great deal of common sense when it came to fixing something that needed fixing . This would usually involve sawing off an offending bit of wood or hitting the problem into submission with a hammer , his constant toil only interrupted by a cup of tea and a fag every five minutes or so. Ceilings would be lowered, cupboards built, cisterns fixed in a flash , all no problem (though not in our house obviously, proper tradesmen don't do their own house, well not until the missus has well and truly nagged them, and only then with a reluctant sigh). Had they let my dad loose on the Berlin wall, it would have been down sometime in the early 70's rather than to that date late in 1989 that it eventually took them to do it. He was a resourceful man, so getting three sets of clubs for us to play golf with that coming Saturday would equally have presented no problem to him. A trip down to the Barras, a market in the East End where you could get everything from a scrubbing brush to a Nuclear Bomb, would soon have provided him with an assorted array of hickory and steel shafted clubs with bags and balls thrown in as part of the deal. The fact that I was considerably smaller than average height for a ten year old also presented "no problem" in getting clubs of my size. The ubiquitous saw and hammer together with some masking tape, produced an assortment of sixty year old wooden shafts and more modern thirty year old steel shafts to fit the wee man – a driver, a three, five, seven and nine iron and an ancient wooden shafted putter that Willie Auchterlonie himself might have used in the late 19th century. All these were held together in a small tartan pencil bag, which also contained an assortment of balls and tees. My brother was equipped with a varied selection of shiny and rusted steel shafted clubs in a natty green leather Greban golf bag and we were away.

I wish I could recall my very first shot, but I can't. What I do remember is the first hole being some 195 yards uphill, but I only discovered that some time later. To a four foot nothing 10 year old it looked a formidable par 4 and I recall regularly hitting my drive straight up the middle , just over a ridge half way to the hole , then giving it a dunt with a 3 iron short, chipping on and 2 putting for a nice opening 5. I could do this with reasonable regularity, occasionally sinking the putt for a 4. I very quickly came to the conclusion that this was a game I enjoyed. This was very much in contrast to my brother , who from day one was able to fashion the most oddly shaped slice I have ever seen. A typical drive from him would start off straight for some 100 yards then take a sharp right at almost 90 degrees for the next 60. Aiming 60 yards left to compensate would either result in a die straight shot into the rough on the left or 100 yards straight followed by a sharp right at almost 90 degrees for the next 100 to finish in the rough on the right. It was true to say that he was not exactly on speaking terms with the fairway. It was not long before he joined the severely misguided " golf is a good walk spoiled" camp, and did not last out the year, returning to the pursuit of catching defenceless fish and practicing at being a melancholy teenager to the sounds of Leonard Cohen.

Whilst I wasn't surprised at my brother being inept at the game (he didn't play football for goodness sake) I was somewhat taken aback that my dad wasn't very good at it either. He wasn't a tall man, but he was a natural athlete . He was also an excellent footballer . He had been to America and played football semi pro there, just after the war. He was also on Celtic's books briefly but the pay as a plumber was much better – this was well before the days of the overpaid prima donnas remember – so he quit to play junior (semi pro) football instead. To add to his sporting C.V. , he was also an accomplished badminton player. Yet, bizarrely, he struggled to hit the golf ball well. He had a shortish swing, lifted his left heel miles off the ground , and seemed to top it a lot. This puzzled me somewhat, although I soon realised if you only play three times a year, you can't expect too much, no matter how good your hand/eye coordination is or how athletic you might be. Despite these failings in the other members of the family, I was hooked however, and I looked forward to Sunday mornings at Ally Park. The only thing was that Ally Park was some 4 miles away and I couldn't get there without my dad taking me. How would I get better only playing once a week ? Fortunately the answer lay not too far from our house in Longstone Road in the shape of Cranhill Park.

It is of great credit to the City Fathers of Glasgow that there exists a large number of green areas within the "Dear Green Place" to where the inhabitants of the city can pursue various sporting activities, simply take a stroll, or let their dog shit all over the grass where young kids would play with some abandon. (Thankfully people are more aware of their responsibilities these days.) Cranhill Park was a fine example of a place where relaxation could be sought by the masses. It had two bowling greens , where the elderly could socialise and while away a few hours at a leisurely pace . It had four clay tennis courts, with red blaze dust that stained your socks forever . Modern detergents claim to be able to remove all stains, but I'm willing to bet these too would have failed to remove the offending clay from those socks. These courts would be chock a block with kids for three weeks of the year , specifically the two weeks of Wimbledon and the week after , and lay predominantly empty for the other forty nine weeks. It had vast grass spaces where copious games of football could be played at the same time. If you were lucky and you had some big boys playing you could commandeer the flat areas to put your jaikets down for the goalposts. If you didn't have big boys then you would be consigned to the slopes of the park – grass slopes at forty five degree angles which Sir Edmund Hillary would've had trouble conquering. But they were grass, and beautiful to play on. But best of all, Cranhill Park had a pitch and putt course.

There may be more beautiful places to hit a golf ball, but the pitch and putt course at Cranhill Park was a great place for a junior golfer to learn to play golf. Always kept in good condition (though the grass on the fairways could get a bit long), the holes varied in length between 30 to 80 yards and had a variety of uphill, downhill and sidehill lies. For a ten year old boy who could hit all of 100 yards with a very well struck drive, this presented a great challenge and a stiff par of 72. The starters hut consisted of a wee green shed, and was run by a thin man with a club foot who had glasses that were as thick as the proverbial milk bottles. I always thought that a bit ironic – a man with a club foot being in charge of the golf facility and , oh, a note for younger readers, milk used to come in glass bottles, not the wishy washy cartons in existence today. You couldn't set a rocket on Guy Fawkes day out of a milk carton these days, but you certainly could from a robust milk bottle. The cost of play was sixpence (2.5 p) and you were issued with a standard parks 5 iron , putter and a yellow rubber ball with a feeling from it so dull that it was pronounced dead on arrival on opening the box it came in. After my dad had taken us down to play a few times I was fortunate to acquire a paper round which I carried out my deliveries round the streets of Cranhill after school. This provided me with the finance to feed my golfing habit, and I was soon able to go on my own. After a few more games I soon realised that the 5 iron provided was both too big for me and was not particularly good at getting the ball above the slightly too long grass when I was close to the green, so I made my first golfing strategic decision at that point – I asked the thin man with the club foot and the thick milk bottle glasses if it would be okay if I brought my own 7 iron with me. To give the man his due , he agreed, though it probably meant he would have to watch other youngsters like a hawk in case they too claimed "they had brought their own club", whilst making off into the distance with the standard parks 5 iron. I'm glad to say that the change was a success, and the sacrifice in distance (that 80 yard hole took two good dunts to reach with a 7 iron) being made up with added finesse around the greens. Within a year I was breaking par, shooting scores in the mid 60's with some regularity. However good that felt at the time, the switch to the 7 iron had an unfortunate side effect in my long term wellbeing as a golfer. Simply put, I became adept at playing 7 iron pitch and runs, whilst playing a short shot with a more lofted club did not enter my way of thinking. Aficionados of the game will mock and ask why I didn't open the face of the 7 iron as Seve did, but that didn't occur to me. A bank in front with the pin at the back of the green ? Just bash it low into the hill and bounce it up. A bank in front with the pin at the front ? Just bash it with a little less force to bounce short then on to the hill to take the sting out of it. That was fine for a pitch and putt course with no bunkers on it. That was also fine for Ally Park which also displayed a distinct lack of bunkers. But would it be fine for "proper" courses ? Never gave it a thought.

But I was not just learning how to hit golf shots playing on the pitch and putt course. It was also on the pitch and putt course at Cranhill Park that I had one of my first lessons in course etiquette. As noted earlier I was now a bit of a golfer, regularly shooting under (my) par at the grand old age of 11. One grey evening, and for some inexplicable reason (presumably my mum wanted them out the house) , my dad and brother had come down to join me for a game. Whether it was the pressure of playing with them or what I know not, but I wasn't at my best that day and I came on to the last tee at only one under , needing an eagle 2 at the 40 yards par 4 eighteenth to break 70. The thought of not breaking 70 made me angry. I was a regular mid 60's player after all. Seventy was the play of duffers, not me. As I addressed the all important tee shot, my concentration was destroyed by my brother practice chipping his ball which ran past my foot just at the crucial moment of takeaway. I stood back and gave him a look that Monty at his peak would've been proud, and raked his ball back to him in a somewhat aggressive fashion. I went back to addressing the ball, but the spell had been broken. I cut my shot slightly and the ball hit the bank at the side of the green, which with the sidespin already on it made it career down the slope and inevitably towards the fence, which was deemed out of bounds. With the last roll of the ball it toppled into the ditch and under the fence . A two shot penalty, the best I could do would be a six (which indeed it was) and a one over par 73. Clearly this was unacceptable and I did what any self respecting golfer aged 11 would do in this circumstance and threw my club as far as I could. Now let me make it perfectly clear. I followed all the rules that a club thrower should follow: if you are going to throw a club, you throw it forward, so that you don't have to walk back to pick it up; you grunt or yell (or shout some profanity – but I was too young for that) to achieve maximum effect; and you throw it upwards and forwards, so that it goes maximum distance, which it did. In fact I threw it so well and so far that had it been the ball I would've had a chance to make my two. None of this impressed my father, who delivered a sharp skelp to my erse (nether regions) by way of admonishment. This was a fairly rare occurrence – he must've given me a good smack early in my childhood because I had always given him healthy respect, and very rarely gave him cause to repeat the dose. For him to have done it outside, in public at age 11 …..hmmm well, I won't be doing that again I thought. And to be fair, I haven't since . To those who remember me occasionally slamming misbehaving wedges into the ground - that doesn't count – they deserve it for their wickedness, after all.

Chapter 3

Lethamhill – the Glory Years

Come the spring of 1971 I was almost twelve years old and had probably unwittingly presented my dad with a bit of a problem. I was now mad keen on the game, and was now playing at a reasonable level – the 50 barrier for 9 holes at Ally Park had long since been broken and I was regularly shooting in the low forties. My brother on the other hand had drifted away and to be honest I'm sure my dad himself would rather have been playing badminton than being out on a golf course. But , as indicated earlier, really there was no such thing as a problem to my dad. As we came off the course one Saturday afternoon he told me that he had spoken to a pal of his, Tommy Dickson, who would get me into his golf club, the Lethamhill Sunday club, which was part of the Lethamhill municipal golf course . This would help my development (and I guess, get him off the hook at the same time) and help fill my increasing appetite for the game. And so the next day he took me (at the crack of dawn) to meet up with Tommy at Lethamhill. Tommy was one of the nicest men you could ever hope to meet , a cheery soul , and he introduced me to life at the Sunday club, a group of 40 or so keen golfers of varying standards, all of whom loved the game. The norm for these guys was to meet up on Sunday morning at 6 am in the summer to join the queue for the clubhouse opening at 7.30 am in the hope they would get tee off times between 8.30 and 10 am. In the winter you would have the luxury of meeting up at 7am, where the experienced boys would have their flasks of tea ready to keep hypothermia from setting in. Once you had signed in the book to get a tee off time, one of the committee members would get a deck of playing cards and you would pick from the pack to see who you played with. From my point of view it really didn't matter to me who I was drawn with – I was just glad to be there – but there was always a bit of excitement in that draw, particularly as I got a bit older and you hoped you would get drawn with one of the better players. I have to say that I am eternally grateful to Tommy and the rest of the Lethamhill boys. In those days the clubs at the course were men's clubs – women and children not to be seen. To take on a twelve year old was a bit of a novelty, but they made me feel welcome and I fitted right in. During the summer it must've been hard to take as I won more than a few medals given that I was playing every day but nobody seemed to mind, maybe because the handicap convenor was keen to chop anyone's handicap who showed a bit of form.

As I played in those early days some of the guys made it known that they also played on a Saturday and that I would be welcome to join them. Joe Wilson, a sage old man, never off the fairway, always giving good advice. Played off about 17, and probably always played off 17 such was his consistency. His best pal, wee Jimmy Donaldson who played off 23 on a good day, a man who inspired mixed emotions . After hitting a duff shot (which not to be unkind was fairly frequently) he became incredibly frustrated, making grumbling and grunting noises not unlike Muttley from the Wacky Races ("snazzun' frackin' frickan'or words to that effect) and thumping his club on the ground or launching it some ways away. I say he inspired mixed emotions – on the one hand you felt genuinely sorry for him and could feel and share his frustration – on the other hand at times so comical that it was hard not to laugh out loud. Alan Park, a nice guy, a keen golfer, but with a swing like Jim Furyk tripping on acid. Jimmy O'Neill , a mid handicapper who could hit a ball, but lacked consistency. Tommy Davidson, who hit the ball 300 yards, though such was his slice, or power fade as he liked to call it after reading a Jack Nicklaus golf book, that it actually only travelled 200 yards as the crow flies. In such good company my golf was bound to progress.

And progress it did. Lethamhill was a very decent golf course , kept in good condition, particularly for a public course. At five thousand nine hundred yards par 72 it was nearly three times the length of Ally Park and it had bunkers guarding the greens and strategically placed bunkers on the fairways to catch well hit slightly off centre drives (or second shots in my case).With my warm up game on the Saturday, Sunday was the highlight of the week. At the tender age of twelve I prepared properly – bath on a Saturday night, gammon sandwiches and a glass of Lucozade and off to bed by 9pm for the 5 am start on Sunday. It's fair to say that I had a pretty steady game at that point – seldom in the rough (partially due to the fact I didn't hit it far enough) , hit it consistently , and was a bit of a demon on the greens – three footers were rolled in without a thought – that's what you're supposed to do isn't it ? (How I wish I could've said that throughout my career !). Breaking 100 was the target – I'd like to think the ability was there, but when your longest drive is 130 yards it can be difficult. (I did say I was a small boy, and not particularly well built). I was certainly getting close to the target – I remember playing a game at Williamwood, a private course in the South Side of Glasgow that year. My Uncle Jack and Aunt Isa (actually my mother's uncle and aunt) lived just across the road from Hampden Park at the old Cathkin Park where Third Lanark used to play. They were incredibly nice people and I used to love it when we visited their house. Not just because they were incredibly nice people and they treated us very well indeed, but Jack was a golfer, and at the top of a green iron spiral staircase, which led to their attic, lay a selection of golfing paraphernalia. Old wooden clubs, balls, golf books and magazines. Whilst the old yins caught up with their yakking and whatever it was they were catching up with, I'd be up the stairs looking at Jack's collection. So it was a joy when my dad told me that he, my brother and me had been invited to play Jack's course at Williamwood. I had not long started playing at Lethamhill and I remember being very impressed by the lushness of the greens at this private course. I played well that day too, shooting 109. I looked forward to the next time I would play there, and my target would be under 100. The return match came almost exactly a year later, when I was a year older and stronger and hitting it a bit further. I shot 112. Golf , I had quickly learned , can be like that.

In spite of such setbacks , I continued to improve, especially over the summer months when I would play daily, and when the family went on holiday to a caravan in Dunbar on the east coast (a distance of 60 miles today, but a million miles away in those days), I'd play up to three times a day, incurring a wee bit of wrath from my mother , with me leaving the caravan at eight in the morning and her having to send out a search party to drag me back at eleven at night. Thank goodness for the light Scottish summer nights – a golfer's dream. Dunbar also gave me my introduction to links golf, and it still remains my favourite golfing terrain to this day.

Now my normal home course, Lethamhill, may not have been links, but there was only one real drawback to playing there, and that was its location. It didn't have sea views, though you could see the Loch from some holes, and it could get a wee bit muddy in the winter, but that wasn't the problem. To explain its natural inbuilt disadvantage, you need to understand the geography and the demography of the East End of Glasgow. Lethamhill was only 3 miles away from my house in Cranhill and it was thus within easy reach. However, to get there I had to walk through Ruchazie, just across the canal from us (now the M8 motorway) and which was twinned with Beruit until they severed the ties because Ruchazie was a bit too rough for them and they wanted to improve their image. As neighbours, it was commonplace in those days for the young residents of Cranhill and Ruchazie to exchange gifts. Every night at around 7 o'clock , the youths of Cranhill would run across the bridge separating Ruchazie from Cranhill throwing their gifts of sticks, stones and bottles to, or more precisely at , the young Ruchazie residents. Not to be outdone by this show of generosity, once the Cranhill boys had dropped all their gifts off, the boys from Ruchazie would pick up some of the offerings add some of their own and chase the gift bearers back over the bridge. Repeat as necessary until they got fed up or got chased by the polis. Great entertainment for the Mooney household, watching from their kitchen window some 100 yards away. No need for TV when you could watch live action as it happened. And as a by the way, there was no such thing as childhood obesity in those days either. If you were fat and you couldn't run, you got caught and you got a doing until your friends realised what was happening and turned back to bail you out. I remember coming back from the pitch and putt one evening at around seven as a fourteen year old, having misjudged the time. I was greeted by the sight of a classmate of mine, Joseph Docherty, or Joe Doc or we cleverly called him, standing on top of a light blue Ford Anglia car with an iron bar in hand , shouting " Come on you Ruchazie bampots – take me !" With an attitude like that, there was only one place that our Joseph was destined to end up. And that's right, just three years later, at the age of seventeen……he joined the Strathclyde Police. I heard recently that he served his 35 years with Strathclyde's finest with distinction and had now taken his well deserved retirement. Obviously his Cranhill background and training had served him well. I often wondered what would have happened that evening if the officers of the law had appeared at that very moment. We could have been cell mates – Joe with his iron bar and me with my seven iron. "Honest officer I was just playing pitch and putt" may not have been a strong enough alibi to get me off the hook. So, given the relationship between the two camps I was always a bit wary of straying into Ruchazie territory, yes , even a specky twelve year old boy of four foot nothing weighing 80 lbs who would, you would think, present no discernable threat to the citizens of that region. However, the Ruchazie people were "them", not "us" and could perhaps pick on the most peaceable person. You would think that at 6 o'clock on a Sunday morning there would be no real danger, but for all I knew they could be lurking behind some tree somewhere, especially on the darker winter mornings as I ventured through Hogganfield Loch towards the golf course.

To be fair, in all the times I played at Lethamhill, I only came into difficulties on two occasions. Lethamhill, as a public course was frequented by a group of boys who would sell you golf balls that they had found. Sometimes you would recognise a ball you had "lost" some holes earlier after hitting it over a hill on a blind hole. You were sure it was still on the fairway, but……must've rolled into the rough. Aye right – the tell tale signs of the bushes being swept aside as the bandits made off into the trees was a bit of a giveaway as to the real destination of your ball. Buying your own ball back was one thing, but on two occasions I was asked to buy my own club back as being a small boy playing on my own presented an enterprising Ruchazie youngster with some easy prey. Now you could say I should have been a bit braver and thus deserved to be relieved of some cash, especially as the two boys in question were no bigger than I was. But remember I was in a hostile foreign territory, and in any case I was not the best fighter in the world. Not that I got into many fights as a boy, but the ones I did get into I can only remember losing , including my first at age 6, when I lost in a fierce encounter to a 5 year old girl. In my defence, she was exceptionally good at pulling hair. Should the reader perhaps think of relieving me of clubs or money today I should advise a word of caution. I've grown up and learned a lot since then and become a lot more streetwise. So much so that I would now be quite confident of taking on a 5 year old girl head to head in a square go. And I've gone bald somewhat, which gives me a bit of an advantage.

Despite these few episodes, my time at Lethamhill was hugely enjoyable. I learned the meaning of some of the golfing terminology. " Great shot!" when commented after your partner in the fourball played a great shot meant "great shot". The same comment applied to an opponent would mean "Lucky B******". " Bite, bite!" in a professional tournament would mean " I've hit a low checking shot, now just sit nicely by the hole". " Bite , bite !" at Lethamhill level meant "Oh shit I've thinned it – hope it's not going through the trees at the back of the green and on to the main road". I met more good, good people playing golf there. Jimmy Lawrie, who was a gaffer in a factory somewhere in Glasgow, but a true gent who would stop his car at bus stops on rainy days and offer people a lift. He would be looked on as some kind of weirdo today, to be avoided at all costs and reported to the police, but it was community spirit at its best then. Bertie Neill, his wee pal, who I formed a kindred spirit with as he was only four foot nothing as well. He worked at Singers in Clydebank , which was miles and miles away. It took him two buses to get to work. I thought he was daft. Living in Clydebank, as I do now, I <u>know</u> he was daft. (Footnote for those in Clydebank who know where I live – just kidding). Jimmy Chapman and his son James, good guys. John McDowall, who would come off the night shift from boning coos at the meatmarket. Good golfer, rough diamond. Good people as they were, my favourite guy to play with was George McFall.

Not a tall man , he had a good sense of humour and played off a handicap of 5 . He didn't hit it a particularly long way, but was incredibly consistent and had an excellent short game. He was also a member at Bishopbriggs, a private course in the North side of the City. Bishopbriggs at that time was known as Spam Valley, where it was common knowledge among those of us who lived in council houses that the residents of "the Briggs" were living beyond their means in an effort to climb the social ladder. The district there was full of "boat" (purchased, not council) hooses, the likes of which we could only dream of. It said much for the friendship at the Sunday club that he continued to play at Lethamhill for a number of years after joining Bishopbriggs, despite having the opportunity of playing with the higher classes. As he was the best player at the club, my target naturally was to be as good as him. Thus my lifelong ambition to attain a five handicap began there and then.

For a while it looked as if I would meet that ambition in a reasonably short space of time. As I grew and got slightly bigger and stronger , allied to playing with these fine people, my handicap came tumbling down, and by the age of sixteen I had reduced my handicap to ten. The Scottish boys championship that year was allowing boys of handicap of nine and under to apply for the knock out stages, so I wasn't far away from being a force to be reckoned with. Different these days , when boys of sixteen are 6 feet plus, play full time, hit the ball 300 yards and are off scratch at worst. I was a full 5 feet 4 inches by that time, still weighed around 8 stone and my only chance of hitting it more than 200 yards was if I drove it down the motorway rather than the fairway. However, I was improving year on year and surely it would only be a matter of time before I reached the goal of 5 handicap and attain George McFall's legendary status.

Before moving on, just a word to clarify my view of living in Cranhill and Ruchazie. It annoys me somewhat when people misrepresent their upbringing to make out that it was tougher than it really was. In general, Cranhill and Ruchazie at that time were fine places to grow up. Yes, there were some nutters, and I do recall the mother of next door's eighteen year old boy running out onto the street to give him a hand when he got into a fight. Not just with moral support, but to hand him a three foot long sword to assist in his travails. (I'll be willing to bet the unfortunate opponent would never again sneer "Whit ur ye gonny dae ? Ur ye gonny get ye mammy to get me?"). But the vast majority of people I knew were decent hard working people who treated each other with respect and raised their families to do the same. And you can't get better than that.

Chapter 4

Lethamhill – The Lean Years

As every golfer knows, whilst life in general can be a bitch, golf can be the bitch from hell. Times ten. When you think things are going well, that's when it'll come up and bite you in the proverbial whatsits. And so it was with me. During the winter of my seventeenth year , I eagerly looked forward to the spring and the prospect of getting my handicap down to single figures and on inexorably towards the magic number of five. Unlike Florida, the golfing season in Scotland (in terms of competitions to get your handicap cut at any rate) runs only from April to September and its only round about March that the average golfer comes out of his hibernation to commence his golfing quest for that year. Not that I was inactive during the winter months – every Saturday and Sunday come rain, hail or shine (mostly rain and hail) I'd be on the course, but there was no nearby golf range to keep the swing going during the week to maintain maximum perfection. Even if there had been, I doubt I could've afforded it in any case. So come April I made a steady if unspectacular start to the year , with decent rounds but no handicap cut , or indeed handicap rise, as we were still on the old handicap system, but more of that later. However come early May of that year, on my seventeenth birthday, I received a birthday present that would change the course of my golfing career. For on that day of my seventeeth birthday, I received from my parents an appointment to get fitted with a pair of contact lenses. If it was my failing eyesight that had led me into the golfing world in the first place, my newly acquired twenty twenty vision without the aid of spectacles was to lead me into a golfing wilderness. It was not that I had different focus on the golf ball when I wore my contact lenses as opposed to glasses . It was just that now that I could see without the aid of milk bottles dangling in front of my face , I could return to my first love football ,and golf would start to take second place. Or more accurately, I should say third place. Being seventeen and now nearly a manly five foot seven, I could just about get into discos on a Saturday night complete with blue velvet jacket without the dreaded knockback from the bouncers at the door. Instead of a pre Sunday golf game preparation of a bath, gammon sandwich , glass of Lucozade and bed by nine, now I had a game of football, a bath, yes , but then off to the disco until 3am getting two hours sleep before it was time to get up for the Sunday morning round. Many an aspiring athlete's career has come to ruin due to drink and women. Although my golfing career went off the rails in my seventeenth year, I cannot claim this. I have never drunk alcohol (I reasoned I always wanted to keep all my senses about me) and have been spectacularly unsuccessful when it came to chatting up women. Thank God for my wife who was either blind or drunk or blind drunk when she met me. My golfing decline came about not through a combination of the demon drink and loose women (alas) but simply through less golf and less sleep. Of course there was still enough left in the tank to perform creditably on occasions – I reached the final of the singles tournament that year to be beaten by a tall chap called Alan Kidd who played superbly well that day, and I also reached the final of the fourball only to finish up runner up yet again . My partner that day was the aforementioned Alan Kidd, who in local parlance "played like a coo" (English translation per the Oxford Dictionary – cow – an animal that roams fields eats grass and produces milk) . To be fair to him, I didn't exactly set the heather on fire either. Re the aforementioned golfing phrase I've always been fascinated by that piece of golfing terminology. I have never seen a coo playing golf so how can you play like one ? Unless therein lies the tale – coos don't play golf, so they must be bad at it. But why not an elephant then ? Or a giraffe ? Never understood it. As an aside , I love golf's propensity for phrases and sayings . My favourite one is when the rain starts falling (which is pretty frequent in the West of Scotland) and some sage will proffer the saying "Aye , it'll be alright – the wind will blow it through quickly".....conveniently forgetting that there probably some 300 miles of rain clouds behind the ones that the "wind will blow through quickly". Yes, there were a few decent scores that year but my handicap remained at ten, a big disappointment given the rapid improvement seen in the previous four years.

A phrase I hate in golf and indeed any sport is when a player or team is doing well and the consensus of opinion is "and he (or she or they) can only get better". Well, no, he or she or they can actually get worse, and this was certainly true in my case. By next season, I had started university, played for the football team on Saturdays , was still frequenting discos until

3 am and didn't have the saving grace of long summer holidays to catch up on my golf. By the age of 18 and being a student, you were now expected to get a summer job which I did, in the shape of being a waiter in the Colonial Restaurant in Glasgow's High Street, which at that time was a high class Italian Restaurant. They say that golf is a great way to meet different people and I'd go along with that. They say it's also good for business dealings, and in some small way that was true for me also, as golf actually helped me get the job at the Colonial. Some eigthteen months previously, five Turkish waiters from the Colonial (Turkish waiters from an Italian restaurant – how unlikely is that?) turned up on the Sunday morning and asked if they could join our club. I was on the committee at that time and despite the fact that these guys had no real background in golf and nobody knew anything about them, we agreed that they should become members. In saying that one of the great things about golf is that you get to meet a whole lot of different people and different types of character, these guys were the absolute proof. Five guys, all from the same region of Turkey, all friends, all colleagues, but all different. Emin – the head waiter – an absolute gentleman. Nagi – a bit of a ladies man

. Bekir – a mischevious character and Suat and Sedat who looked as if they should be undertakers but had a nice understated sense of humour. These boys indeed brought something different – a ball hit off line and heading towards an unsuspecting golfer would be greeted with a cry of "Watch ! Watch !" and we did have to tell them that spitting at the hole when you missed a putt was not to be found in any of the golfing etiquette books …..and wasn't particularly nice for the person coming along next. They seemed to enjoy the gambling aspect more than the actual golf itself and frequently broke into an excitable exchange in the Turkish language, usually ending in a word that sounded to me like "Moruk". I asked Emin what that word meant in English. He smiled, and being the gentleman he was told me it meant "old man". To this day I am still not entirely certain he told me the truth – but you can be sure I that if I'm ever in Turkey and I see an old man, I won't be calling him "Moruk" in case I get a smack in the mouth for suggesting that he's a wanker. However they did indeed bring a bit of colour to the club and became decent players. Latterly, Nagi, who was the best of them , took great delight in pointing out that he had only been playing for three years and had achieved a handicap of ten whereas I'd been playing forever and my handicap was eleven (the committee had taken pity on me and gave me an extra stroke by that time) . Aye cheers mate, thanks for that.

     Much as I'd enjoyed the Lethamhill Sunday club my time there was coming to an end. At age eighteen , my dad told me he knew a member of Crow Wood, a private course in Muirhead some 6 miles away, and that he would propose me to become a member. At that time there was a waiting list of some three years to get in (changed days eh?) and as I had passed my driving test, getting to the course would not be a problem. So the forms were filled in, and indeed three years later , with my golf still in some decline, I became a member of Crow Wood Golf Club.

Chapter 5

Crow Wood Private Members Club

Becoming a member of a private golf club in those days was a big deal. Unlike today where you apply, you pay your cash , and you are in, there was much more status afforded to the process of becoming a member. For a start, you had to be proposed and seconded by members of the club (some clubs required even more members to recommend you than that). You and they completed the form which would get you on the waiting list. This happened to be three years for Crow Wood, but waiting lists of ten years was not uncommon for some courses. When your time came, you would be invited to appear before the committee where they would ascertain if you were a fit and proper person to join their golf club. Questions like "where do you come from, what's your golfing experience" would be asked before a thorough check of your teeth to make sure you were healthy. In reality it was not so bad an experience – the days of "blackballing" someone because the committee didn't like the look of you had just about gone, but some of the old practices remained. In retrospect, its maybe not a bad idea to revive – it allows the "newbie" to meet with the people who help run the club and vice versa, but to the non golfer it does smack of golf being stuck in the dark ages. Whatever the thought, I turned up in my best (only) suit and must've came across as a decent sort because my application was approved and I was in (after paying my joining fee of course).

I was twenty one by now and was in my first year of training to be a Chartered Accountant. Now let me just say right here that the image of Chartered Accountants portrayed by Monty Python of dreadfully dull boring people is completely misguided. Okay, we may not be the most dynamic risk takers in the world, but there were quite a few golfers among the CA fraternity when I started my training , so , for that reason alone, they can't be all that bad. Among them was the Club Champion at Turnberry, Gordon Rodger , who like my previous icon, George McFall , played off 5. So I rest my case . Dull ? Can't possibly be. But I digress - by the time I arrived at Crow Wood my handicap was still eleven, though if truth be told, it should've been nearer 16, as the football and discos were still taking priority. To be fair, there were times in my last years at Lethamhill where I showed occasional signs of returning to my previous golfing ability. Three years earlier, two younger guys, Steven Phinn and George Dobie had joined the club. Aged around 15, these boys played off 5 and 7 respectively, altogether eclipsing the previous young gunslinger Mooney by quite some distance. When the boys came up at first, they were accompanied by Steven's father, Willie, who it transpired, had taught Steven (and latterly George) from an early age. Steven had a particularly good golf game and went on to become an assistant professional at Cowglen before going the way of so many before him, scunnered at hardly playing golf and sitting in a shop all day. He quit after a couple of years and was largely lost to the game, which given his talents was a great shame.

When I started to struggle with my game I concluded that it must be something technical, conveniently ignoring the fact I was spending less time playing, and given that Willie Phinn had been so successful in teaching his son, I asked him to give me some lessons. He was my first real "coach". Yes , I had a number of lessons prior to this but they were all unofficial….. when I was going off the rails a bit

I received plenty of advice from various people in the Sunday Club . Joe Wilson's tips were pretty much spot on, but others - swing too flat , make it more upright being a common theme – could well have done more harm than good. Missed that three foot putt, having holed the previous nine out of ten ? Your stance is too wide and you "pop" the putt. Narrow your stance and stroke it. It is a wonderful thing in golf that all golfers, no matter what their handicap, are experts in the golf swing and most are only too willing to impart their knowledge on the unsuspecting victim. Well intentioned, but truly beneficial in the long term? Probably not. Anyway Willie, whilst not playing the game himself for quite sometime, had a good eye for a golf swing. More than that, he was an incredibly interesting character, a bit of an eccentric. A chain smoker, he could talk endlessly about everything and anything. In all honesty, I was reasonably bright at school , and was offered the chance to go to St.Mungo's Secondary school , which at the time, was a school for "high achievers". I turned down the opportunity – after all St. Gregory's school in Cranhill was just 5 minutes walk away from my house, and I could go home at lunchtime to get pieces (sandwiches) made by my mum. To get to St.Mungos I would've had to get a bus and get up an hour earlier , eat school dinners (not good for a picky wee boy) and get home an hour later. To me the decision was , in American speak, a no brainer , but on hearing this tale, Willie chastised me for making that decision . These schools he said, taught you to have what he called a "superiority complex". It's what got you on in life. Some thirty years later I read a book by Doctor Bob Rotella, the celebrated golf psychologist, virtually saying you had to have a "superiority complex" to become the best golfer you could be. He may have been an eccentric, but Willie was no fool.

He was also a good teacher. At University I had joined the golf section, and at practice, a prominent Scottish Golfer, Billy Lockie, would go round the practice nets giving advice . I think he spent 30 seconds with me. Some might say he reckoned he couldn't improve perfection. Others would probably argue he couldn't be bothered spending time with a ten handicap chopper when he had boys of scratch material to work with. Willie had no such qualms about spending time. We would spend a couple of hours at a spare bit of ground at Ally Park with him patiently correcting my action whilst at the same time imparting knowledge about just how much tea there was in China and other such worldly topics. And indeed the coaching sessions started to work. Not all the time mind you , as I remember a lesson on the Saturday morning being the (partial) reason for a drive off the first tee on the Sunday morning that went all of three feet, and resulted in a 9 & 8 gubbing in my singles tie. In the main, however, he brought me back from the blight of poor golf that I was suffering from at that time.

Despite the fact that I suspect he was privately educated (he never actually told me), Willie had a deep distrust of people and places getting above themselves. When I joined Crow Wood , I thought that I'd better give this a good shot (having shelled out a good few bob to join), and I asked Willie if he wouldn't mind doing some extra lessons. I think he quite liked Crow Wood, despite its manor like clubhouse and stately drive up to it from the Stepps Road. People there were more "normal" than he thought they may have been and it amused him when my Morris Marina's headlight caved in due to the rust around it as it stood beside the other , posher cars in the car park. He agreed to the extra lessons, and after two years I had got my handicap down to seven, thanks to Willie's teaching prowess, some extra time spent on the range (Crow Wood has an excellent practice facility) and the fact that whilst I still went to discos on a Saturday night (after golf lesson Saturday morning and football game Saturday afternoon), my tee off time on a Sunday was around 1 o'clock, and I was able to get a good eight hours sleep as opposed to the two hours when playing at the Sunday Club at Lethamhill.

My stay at Crow Wood was destined to be a short one however. At 21 I had met Maria at the Ultrateque disco in Glasgow and after the first meeting I knew she could certainly be "the one", particularly as no other girls would go out with me. Two years later we were due to be married and on the 17th September 1983 we were. I remember it as if it was yesterday…..and you know what a terrible day yesterday turned out . (Les Dawson circa 1973). Anyhow, married we were, and one week later , just back from honeymoon in Blackpool (I know how to treat a girl) I was due to play in the singles final at Crow Wood.

Looking back, getting to the singles final at Crow Wood was a bit of an achievement for me. Yes, I had reached the singles final at Lethamhill – but there was only 30 odd entrants and just 4 games to get to the final. At Crow Wood there were over 200 entrants and 7 or 8 games to get there. I remember beating a 3 handicap player at the last hole in the semis (was 4 up with 4 to play, nearly blew it) and my opponent in the final was an 18 handicap golfer called John , whose surname I can't quite remember . John was a nice guy , but as a golfer was a hockey player first and foremost. He had a hockey like swing , short back and short through , hit it very consistently, and as he told me later, got up early every morning to practice his short game. The final was to be over 36 holes, and I was giving him eight shots in each of the eighteen holes (three quarters of handicap difference in those days) and if I thought I was going to be in trouble as I lost the first hole, this was confirmed as he finished the first eighteen six up. Nonetheless, in my own naïve and optimistic way, I reckoned it was not over till it's over and I played away steadily (mixed with some brilliance if you don't mind me saying) and by the thirty fifth hole we were all square. The seventeenth hole at Crow Wood was stroke index 5 , so although I had clawed his lead back I was by no means favourite. Nonetheless I hit a great drive down the middle, a sublime 5 wood (which I remember had a lovely deep red wooden head on it) to four feet. John on the other hand had played his usual game. A drive down the middle, a shot just short of the green and a chip on to 12 feet. He then missed the putt, which gave him a five, net four.

Did you ever witness the famous "Duel in the Sun" at Turnberry in 1977 between Tom Watson and Jack Nicklaus ? Students of the game will recall an excellent contest between two of the world's best golfers, both men producing breathtaking golf , neck and neck until the 17th hole in the last round. Nicklaus , you will remember, had a 4 foot putt for birdie, which he putted and missed (he later said he hit the putt just as he wanted to – it just didn't go in). I was that man. I hit my 4 foot putt with my Ram Zebra putter, and just like my kindred spirit, Big Jack, it grazed the left side of the hole, and much to my amazement, stayed out. The strange thing is, I reckon I haven't hit many better putts – for a pressure situation I remember having no nerves and being confident it would go in. But it didn't. And instead of being one up with one to play we were all square going down the last. To cut a long story short, we both scabbed it down that thirty sixth hole and both recorded bogey 6's at the long par five. The game finished in a half , and the rules dictated that another 36 holes would be played the following Sunday.

What can I tell you about the rematch ? Well, after the first eighteen, I was, yes you've guessed it, six down. In the afternoon, just as the previous week, I clawed it back bit by bit and by the time we reached the last hole (our seventy second) I was one down. John played the hole well. After three hits he lay some 15 feet away from the hole. I on the other hand, had flown my third shot over the green. I indicated earlier that a chip and run was my standard short shot. This was no use to me in this situation, having to clear some rough and get up and over a bank to get to the flag . I opened a wedge and played the shot. The ball flopped beautifully on to the green, and although I couldn't see the result, I could see the look on John's friends faces (who had come out to support their man) and I knew it had gone in the hole. " Thanks " I said, as one of them magnanimously mumbled "Good shot"….at least I think that's what he said. It could equally have been "Lucky Bar Steward", as the two of them sound very similar.

Whichever it was, the ball had indeed gone in the hole for a birdie four. Pleased as I was, I wasn't overly excited. John still had his 15 footer to win the match, and my excellent shot would be in vain. Not that I was worried as such, but if I had been I needn't have. I don't think I've ever seen a fifteen footer miss a hole by quite so much, and the match was , once again , all square.

We went into the clubhouse and enquired what the protocol was to decide the tie. The committee in their wisdom decreed that another 36 holes would be too much for anyone. We would play another 18 holes, and on to sudden death if tied .

I wish this story had a happy ending, but it doesn't , at least not for me, that is. I said earlier that I couldn't remember what John's surname was. If I ever needed to know it, all I would need to do is go to the Crow Wood trophy cabinet and look at the name of the 1983 singles champion. John , steady as ever , and true to form , went six up in the third match. As it was an eighteen hole event, the match thus finished on the thirteenth (or eighty fifth to be precise) .

It wasn't long after that that I left Crow Wood. Not in some fit of pique for being robbed of the singles title (which I wasn't – well played John) but by then I was married and we had moved over to Old Kilpatrick, some 25 miles west of Crow Wood. In my two years at Crow Wood I had occasionally gone back to see my friends at the Lethamhill Sunday club, but now, staying in the Clydebank area I was gone for good.

Chapter 6

Milngavie Golf Club – The First Eighteen

Sometimes , though maybe not often enough, Lady Luck smiles on you and deals you a good hand in the poker of life. Sometimes this happens in the most unlikely of places at the most unlikely time. And so it was with me and my introduction to Milngavie Golf Club. As noted earlier, having left university I commenced employment in the real world with a Chartered Accountancy firm, Thornton Baker, who were based in West George Street in Glasgow. I remember being asked as a six or seven year old what I wanted to be when I grew up. Without a word of a lie, I can remember my answer, clear as day . "I don't know" I said, "but I don't want to be a Chartered Accountant". Well when it came to choosing a career some fourteen years later, Lady Luck must've been out to lunch, because, having not given it much thought, I drifted into accountancy. To be fair I was always good with numbers, and accountants were supposed to be good with numbers (though when I consider the banking crisis and various frauds sometimes I wonder) , so it seemed to me maybe I was wrong all those years ago, and I accepted the contract. Honest to God, life as a Chartered Accountant isn't as dull as some would make out – you are well trained and learn good disciplines, which if adhered to, and most do, will lead to well run businesses. However, I confess the audit profession wasn't my first love, but it was in this environment that I received my next golfing break as Lady Luck returned from lunch.

I was in the office at West George Street discussing golf with a fellow CA trainee, Bob Smith. We had played at an office outing the week before (just a thought – but do gay golfers reveal their sexuality for the first time at a golf outing ?) and were catching up with tales of the days events, as golfers tend to do. Not only was Bob a good guy, but he played off a single figure handicap, which earned him additional respect. As we chatted I told him that Maria and I were about to buy a flat in the Clydebank area and I'd be moving there in six months time or so. On hearing this, he said that he'd get me an application form for Milngavie Golf Club, where he was a member. Without knowing anything about it , other than Bob's recommendation (no such thing as websites in those days) I readily agreed, the form was completed, and eighteen months later I was in.

Before I joined, Bob had told me that Milngavie Golf Course was the finest course in the region. Well, since my first viewing of it , to this day some nearly thirty years later and having played all the courses in the area , I have had no cause to disagree with his assessment. This is said with no disrespect to any of the other courses in the area, but located at the start of the West Highland Way in Milngavie , the scenery is stunning and the course layout, originally designed by Willie and Laurie Auchterlonie and amended later by James Braid (though not too much) it presents a challenge to any golfer, despite not being overly long in length. There are fewer finer places to be on a sunny summer evening, no question.

I was however, still playing football, this time for Cambria, a team of Strathclyde University graduates and my golfing season was really restricted to the three summer months plus a bit of evening golf where I could manage, and Maria (bless her) let me. Like Bob, I joined the "dawn patrol", a group of keen golfers who as the name suggests , started early morning. For a man who was brought up with 5am starts for the Lethamhill Sunday Club, this presented no real challenge and I still have vivid pictures in my mind of the dew on the lush green fairway at the first hole on many a sunny Saturday morning from those early years.

So much for the scenery and the ambiance of Milngavie Golf Club – how was the golf progressing ? Well, it was holding up pretty well. Living at the other side of the world from Willie Phinn , my golfing mentor (who sadly, just a few years later died at his son's wedding) I now only saw him occasionally for a catch up in the world's affairs and a quick eye over my swing. However, I was still playing decent golf, and Bob Smith and I reached the semi finals of the fourball, only to be pipped by the low handicap pairing of Graeme Smith and Ken Miller. I don't think Bob ever forgave me for three putting the thirteenth when we were all square, though in my defence, the green was devilishly fast that day, and my well struck second shot finished twelve feet past the hole. My equally well struck first putt finished a further twelve feet past the hole going in the opposite direction, and I failed with the return putt, a decisive moment in the match. Perhaps in search of a better golfing partner, Bob emigrated to Portsmouth and the sunny climes of the South of England just two months later, though he used the excuse of a better paid job to cover the real reason.

The following season saw some changes in my golfing pattern. Paul, our first born arrived, and I quit the dawn patrol seeking a longer lie (Paul permitting) and the company of mid morning /afternoon golfers. I was still playing football in the winter months, and with a reduced playing schedule allied to no longer receiving coaching from the excellent Willie Phinn, my game started its inevitable decline. The occasional excellent round was now heavily outnumbered by the vast majority of mediocre rounds, and my handicap rose steadily upwards. Milngavie presents a stern challenge if you miss a green, particularly left or right. A delicate pitch over a bunker or grassy knoll (I'm sure Lee Harvey Oswald used to practice there as some of the greens were more difficult to hit than a president) from a tight lie is normally your fate, and having been brought up on chipping and running, there were many Waterloo moments facing me , and many times I was Napoleon rather than Nelson.

And thus, after a few short years, my handicap had eased ever upwards and by 1994 at age of 35, just when I should have been hitting the peak of my golfing career, I found myself with a handicap of 12. Not too terrible you may think, but to a man who had reached that handicap (going in the correct direction) some 20 years earlier this did not exactly fill me with delight. However, I did console myself with the words of Willie Phinn, who once after a rare unproductive lesson, commented that some people catch on later than others. Whilst I'm sure he didn't mean me as I'm obviously a quick learner, I did think that my best golfing years were yet to come, but I realised that they weren't going to come by themselves, and at that point I thought I'd better do something to make my golfing aspirations come to fruition.

It was thus that I found myself going to Clydebank and District golf club, just two minutes down the road from my house to visit the golf pro there, David Pirie. At that time, Milngavie did not have a pro attached to it. The Collinson's had tried some years before, but could not make a living from it. Bob Collinson was at Windyhill Golf Club and latterly at

Bearsden driving range. I could have gone there, but had heard that David at "the Hardgate", as Clydebank and District is known, was a good teacher and I decided to give him the chance to work with one of the district's up and coming golfers (that would be me, just in case you weren't following the story). David , I found, is an affable man and was easy to get on with. He is indeed a good coach, with a sound knowledge of the golf swing, and I got on well with him. As I found out however, he does have one serious character defect (he is a keen Rangers supporter and takes up half the lesson talking about his beloved Gers) but nobody's perfect. After a couple of lessons, I began to feel the benefit, but all too soon the season ended without making a significant dent to my handicap. However I vowed to have one or two more lessons the following year to keep the improvement going.

And indeed, come early the next season I did have one or two lessons. However much I felt I was progressing though, I wasn't going to have too many more. Whilst not exactly being poor, our family had been completed by our second arrival Stacey in 1990, and as many will know, a young family is a cash hungry animal and I didn't want to spend my hard earned on too many lessons. It was at that point that Lady Luck smiled down upon me again – I became an Open Championship winner at St.Andrews.

Now you may well think that the winner of the Open Championship in 1995 at St.Andrews was one Sir Nicholas Faldo, and I'm sure his name is indeed inscribed on the Claret jug for that year. However, a far more significant event in golfing history occurred that July on the Old Course. For it was there , at that very same event , that I won a competition run by Golf Monthly. "Enter the Golf Monthly Prize Draw" the notice proclaimed. Being a free competition, and being a true Scotsman , I naturally entered it, putting my name and address on the competition postcard, and slotting putting it into the entry box. I then left to watch Sir Nick win the golf, and thought no more about it. Until that is, three weeks later , when a package arrived at the door, courtesy of Golf Monthly. I opened the package, and there contained within it , lay a very nice putter. On the hozzle of putter was the name "Scotty Cameron". Now I've always been reasonably well up on all things golf, but at that point I had never heard of Scotty Cameron. World famous in the putter market now obviously, but brand new to the UK in 1995. It was the following week, when reading my Golf Monthly , that I saw an article or advertisement for Scotty Cameron putters – retailing at £140 . Good grief, I had won a fortune ! Realising that this putter was too good for the likes of me, I took the putter down to David at the Hardgate and traded it in for £100 of lessons. I took 3 or 4 more lessons by the end of that summer and began to see a distinct improvement.

It has to be said that my handicap didn't shoot down right away. For a start, I was still involved in the football with Cambria. Now aged 36, I was the third team player manager. I say player....by that time my calf muscles had packed up on me , a product no doubt of earlier years pounding the streets to keep fit, and I thus only played when we were short of players. Which, unfortunately was pretty often – if the first and second teams had call offs they called on my players and I would be forced to play (or more precisely hobble). This lasted for a further three years until at the age of thirty nine I gave it up and alas, haven't played since. This decision did however, release more time to play golf, and allied to David's fine tuition, my handicap came down steadily and by the time 2004 came around, I was back down to a handicap of seven, for the first time in twenty years. The lifetime goal of a handicap of five was starting to become a distinct possibility.

It was then Lady Luck turned her back on me once more. I had the misfortune to have an unfortunate conversation with a man called John Hamilton, or the career wrecker as I like to call him.

Chapter 7

The Committee Years

I had known John Hamilton almost since I had started golf at the Milngavie Golf Club. Along with his cousin David, he was one of the keen enthusiasts of the dawn patrol when I first joined (and indeed is to this day) and he and I became very good friends. A very consistent golfer, he played off 6 and is one of the few golfers whose enthusiasm for golf and all things golf exceeds my own. In his house he has a " Baxter Collection" – a collection of prints of golf holes painted by the renowned artist Graham Baxter. If John visits a course where Baxter has painted a hole, and he happens to birdie that hole, the print is purchased and adorns the Hamilton household wall the very next evening. Fortunately , his wife Lynda also plays golf, and is thus very understanding of John's enthusiasm, though I'm sure she secretly hopes he doesn't birdie any more to add to the collection of six or so already hanging proudly around the house.

Although I quit the dawn patrol some years back, John and I still played some golf together. Together with his cousin David and another friend, Andy Murrison we would go on golf away days two or three times a year and occasionally catch up with each other for a round at Milngavie. These games away would normally be organised by John, who is a born organiser. During the day and sometimes night, he works as a Head Administrator in the Greater Glasgow Health Board. For those who think that this is an oxymoron – i.e. organisation and the Health Board can't be part of the same sentence, I would just argue that we as a nation and generation have become people who continually focus on the 1% of things that go wrong and ignore the 99% of things that go right. Let me assure you, the man is an organiser. When the phone goes, if my wife answers and it's "that bad man John Hamilton" on the other end of the line, I know that a great golfing day out has been well and truly sorted.

So it came to me as no surprise therefore, when playing a game sometime in 2004 (I don't recall the date but I do recall wandering down the fifteenth fairway with him when the bombshell was first broached) that John revealed to me that he'd been nominated for the Vice Captaincy of the club in 2005 and would thus become Club Captain in 2006. The only problem was, he said, that as he'd committed to be Junior Convenor (a role he had only just taken on the previous year) he would need to find somebody else to take on this important position within the club . What did I think ?

What did I think ? My first thought was "Good luck with that one mate". My second thought wasn't quite as harsh as that and I found myself saying, "if you can't find someone else to do it then ok, I'll give it a go". I had been at the club for eighteen years by that time and had managed to avoid committee duties. Someone has to do it, otherwise the club doesn't function. My son Paul, who had joined two years previously as a junior (not an entirely enthusiastic one it had to be said – the game's frustrations weighed too heavily on his shoulders) was, at sixteen still in the junior section and I thought that maybe of all the committee jobs that was going, just maybe this would be the one for me to do, and at the same time, encourage my boy to get better at the game. He latterly built himself a nice swing, which will stand him in good stead for years to come and get him through the occasional game he now has, but like his old dad, loved football and thus left Milngavie at 21, when his aforementioned old dad stopped paying his subscriptions.

It is interesting that whilst John recalls our conversation going down the fifteenth, his version is slightly different from mine. He remembers the chat as going "you've been here eighteen years Brian, it's about bloody time you did something for the club !" It should be pointed out however, that John is some two years older than me , and at that age is thus an unreliable witness, and his testimony should thus be discounted.

These days, people say to me that I'm a born committee man. Nothing could be further from the truth. It is true that at the age of 15 I became treasurer of the Lethamhill Sunday Club and at 16 its Club Captain (probably only noteworthy for the time when I put up a notice on the noticeboard with the word SEX in 6 inch high letters, followed by the reminder that their annual fees were due….it worked, I got the cash in) but I would much rather just play and let someone else get on with it. Nonetheless there comes a time when you need to stand up and be counted, because as I say that's how these things work.

It helped me enormously that the previous incumbent of the junior convenor's role was indeed the aforementioned organiser. Prior to him becoming junior convenor (no disrespect to others that preceded him) the junior section at Milngavie was in a much depleted state, with less than 30 members . Within two years, John had persuaded the committee to cut the fees for juniors and with his time and enthusiasm (I remember him clearing the greens of water so that a junior final could go ahead, this being just one of the "over and above the call of duty" tasks he did) had doubled the numbers so that by the time I came into the job we had a more healthy number of 55 juniors. I helped him with his last 6 months of junior convenorship and being the organised man that he is, he ensured that the handover to the new boy was a smooth as the proverbial baby's bum.

My three year sentence as junior convenor was actually a very pleasurable one. The section grew to a record number of 165 members in that space of time, largely thanks to John's wise revision of the fees but also to the help and involvement of a good few members and parents of the children, too many to name (you know who you are), who helped run the teams, and helped out with the various competitions (official and unofficial) that we organised. I'd like to think that our attitude to the job helped – the juniors were treated as proper members and the competitions for the younger ones were made fun. Winners of the competition (kids love competition) would win golf balls, and there always seemed to be enough prizes that everyone would win something , even if they weren't first. For the older juniors, we got the rules changed so that they could play off the gents medal tees . To me this made much sense - they were hitting it further than most of the members for goodness sake – and gave them more encouragement. We attended all the medals and it felt like a proper club, with the boys and girls telling their tales of their round at the end, and generally having a good time.

Perhaps the most difficult aspect of the job was dealing with the clubmaster at the time, Paul Wade. Paul was a bit old school, where children and indeed full adult members should be seen and not heard. Whilst appreciating that standards had to be maintained , there are ways and means of doing this, and mine differed from Paul's. That is not to say that discipline was unimportant and for example, I suspended two boys for 3 months for constantly practicing on the course . Due to this they subsequently left , which from my point of view was a pity because they were just keen , and not bad as such. I hope they went on to another course and pursued their golfing career. I also hope that they learned that sometimes you just have to toe the line, whether you like it or not. However, the fact was that I was more tolerant of youthful exuberance than Paul and indeed some of the other members were. Had he had his way, two of our boys, the twins Ben and James Williams would have been banned and probably hung, drawn and quartered, due to the "lip" they would give him when he was laying down his law. What he saw as "lip" I saw as a bit of harmless banter, like adults would naturally have, and it's perhaps the greatest testimony to my time as junior convenor that both are still valued members at Milngavie and that James is now the Junior Convenor. The number of juniors has dropped off significantly since my days as convenor, but with James at the helm the trend is being reversed, and I'm sure will grow back to full strength in the near future. That group of boys has also seen two of them go on to the committee in match and handicap and finance, further strengthening the club.

My role in helping with committee tasks didn't just stop at being junior convenor. In another committee inspired night, John asked me to do a wee turn at his Captain's Prizes dinner. Round about that time I had started to do a comedy routine on the odd occasion, and part of this was singing a song I had written called "Pissin'", a song about the amount of rain falling in the West of Scotland. He asked me if I could sing it, but add a verse specifically for the Milngavie Golf Club. I did, and the verse turned out to be very prophetic. It went

Well nowadays I play some golf at Milguy,
But ever since I've been here, well it's never been dry,
Be the season be summer or winter, result is always the same,
Aw the medals are cancelled, cause it's always pissin' a rain.

On that very day, on Captains Prizes Day, it was indeed pissin'. It was battering it down and blowing a gale into the bargain. I was one of the last out, but I was playing well, putting through puddles, head down against the wind, the lot. My head hurt with the vast amount of concentration required to hold a score together in such testing and trying conditions. But hold it together I did, and as I came off the eighteenth I felt good. 74 less 9 for a net 65 and what was surely a winning score. As I approached the clubhouse I was met by match and handicap convenor, Euan McGregor. "Good score today Brian ?" he enquired. "Yes indeed" I replied, "so good that it's the winning score, no doubt about it". "Pity" he said, "we've cancelled the medal, it's too wet". I can tell you that I nearly told John to shove his Captain's dinner there and then, but then my ego kicked in the lure of playing in front of a captive audience proved too strong, and the song was duly sung, and I can tell you, with some feeling. On the plus side, I was rewarded with a handicap cut of 0.6 for my troubles…..

However good a score that may have been that day, it is true to say that in general, whilst I was spending more time at the golf course during those three years , I was actually spending less time playing golf. In addition, early on in my committee stint I had stopped my lessons with David Pirie. I had reached the club championship last 16 and was looking for a lesson to top up my game beforehand. He couldn't give me the half hour I was looking for, and I decided if he couldn't make the time and be at my beck and call when I needed him, I'd go it alone ……a big mistake as it turned out. In the three years on the committee my handicap drifted from seven back up to ten.

When my three years as junior convenor was up , I decided that I would get my game back in shape again. At the young age of just fifty , I reckoned my peak was still to come. After all, you just can't beat experience , and I enlisted the help of Gary McFarlane, a good coach who had been at World of Golf and Loch Lomond and who was in between assignments. I first met Gary when we hired him to give lessons to the juniors as part of the coaching programme we had organised, but he then moved to nearby Clober Golf Club when a position became available there. I went to him for two years, and got my handicap back down to eight.

Just as things were getting better and I was heading towards my goal, Lady Luck turned her back on me once more. The Vice Captain of Milngavie at the time, Gordon Fairbrother, was on the lookout for a Vice Captain for the following year. Having asked two hundred and thirteen other potential candidates, and having had the bottom of the barrel well and truly scraped, he asked me, in some desperation, if I would consider the role. I gave it some thought, but knew that the time commitment to this onerous job would be too much for me, so I offered a counter suggestion – no. He accepted this, as he had accepted the other two hundred and thirteen rejections , but asked me if I would consider being on the greens sub committee. My answer was a resounding and less than enthusiastic "if you can't get anyone else, come back to me".

And of course , he did. After all, no one in their right mind would want to be greens convenor, would they ? If things go well, nobody notices it, and those who do notice it , assume it's because of the good weather we've been having recently. If things aren't quite as they should be….and because they've cut their grass at one time or another, there's over four hundred green keeping experts at the golf club, each of them with their own view of what's wrong with the course and how we should be doing a thousand and one different things to improve the course. Having said that, even as I write , I've just completed my stint as firstly assistant greens convenor and then then greens convenor. I'd like to think I've made some difference – we employed an apprentice green keeper to bring numbers up to a level that allowed the greens staff to do extensive drainage work and invested heavily in machinery to allow us to get the greens and the course in general the way we would like it. We are fortunate to have Wallace Wilson and his staff at Milngavie. They know what they are doing, although Wallace would laugh at the suggestion that we have invested heavily in machinery. Like all green keepers he has statistics to show that his club spends a lot less than other clubs, and I'm sure he's right. That Loch Lomond club up the road does tend to spend a bit more, but then again they charge their members twenty thousand pounds a year in membership. Again, older members in the club will scoff at my suggestion that the course has improved recently, remembering the days when the course was in much better condition and the ball rolled further on the beautifully manicured fairways….. or was it just that they were a bit younger then and could hit it further ? Or could it be that back then Global Warming hadn't taken hold, depositing, as it does now , even more copious amounts of water upon us than in times gone by. And yes, Wallace has statistics to show that that's the case.

Getting back to the real issue , however, I've found , that as previously, my time on the committee has resulted in some cost to my golf game. And no wonder. Precious time spent on committee meetings could have been spent on the course or on the practice area. Due to time restrictions I also stopped going to Gary McFarlane and my handicap rose from eight to ten. I am firmly of the view that applications to prospective committee members should carry the following golf health warning "Joining the committee can seriously increase your handicap". You may think this is my excuse for poor play. In truth, you are probably correct…… but I've got the statistics to prove it.

I've talked a lot about handicaps so far . Just one more quick observation on the handicap system. The seven handicap I achieved in 2002 was, in my view, better than the seven handicap I achieved back in 1983. How so ? In the old days, your handicap was a measure of how good a golfer you could be, in that if you scored lower than par (or standard scratch to be specific) your handicap came down by the number of strokes you beat par by. So if you were playing off a handicap of nine and shot net two under, your handicap would be reduced to seven. If you played badly after that your handicap didn't go up, until, at the end of the year, the committee reviewed the handicaps. If you had some scores near your best they would probably leave it. If your other scores were higher they would give you an increase. Contrast that with today, where a score of two under par would get you down by 0.4 (for mid handicap players) and for every score over par (or buffer zone for the specifically minded) you go up 0.1. Today's handicap thus is a measure of how good a golfer you are on average, by taking you down more slowly and also giving you automatic increases when playing less well. I make no comment on the differences other than to say it was more pleasurable playing in the old days. You did not have the pressure of trying to make the buffer zone, failing by a stroke, then feeling bad afterwards because your handicap had gone up.

I'm not saying the new system is bad…..I'm just saying.

Chapter 8

The Open

Much as I love golf, I have already documented that my first love in sport is football. However, since the age of ten , my favourite week of the whole year is not on the occasion of the Champions League final or even the World Cup final, but the week of the Open Championship. Now let me make this very clear. When I talk about the Open Championship I am taking about the Open Championship , not the British Open , for there is no such thing. I am not a violent man (witness my beating by a five year old girl some fifty years ago) but in my view anyone who calls the Open the "British" should be castrated or at the very least punched in the face. This especially applies to television commentators, who are paid to know better.

Rant over. I first became aware of The Open in 1969, which was a good year for British Golf. Firstly , and most importantly, I started the game in that year, and secondly, Tony Jacklin won the Open at Royal Lytham & St. Annes. It was on the TV and I watched all that I could of it. In those days however it wasn't the wall to wall coverage that you get these days. No – despite the fact that it was on the BBC and there were no adverts, just as things would be getting interesting there would be a break whilst Auntie Beeb switched transmission to cover the cricket and the Test Match from Lords or Trent Bridge or wherever. What on earth were they thinking about ? Peter Alliss , in his excellent book Bedside Golf, relates the time he was sent a letter from an irate Scots golfer , complaining about cricket interrupting the golf, which I wish that I could copy here. In these times however, it would probably be deemed both racist and homophobic , but I can only tell you the writer deemed cricket not to be a real sport and those who played it and watched it were of an effeminate nature from South of the Border and they should take it and place the whole thing up a delicate place of the anatomy. I must confess, I shared his views, as the whole event of the Open had me hooked, though it was not until ten years later that I attended an Open in person.

The year was 1979, and by then I was a student at Strathclyde University . I happened upon a notice on the Golf Board requesting volunteers to man (or person) the scoreboards for that years Open, which was being held at

Royal Lytham & St.Annes, near Blackpool. Thinking this would be a good idea, i.e. get paid to watch golf , I applied and was accepted. Down I went, and though I didn't get on to the course as part of my job (I was allocated duties in the press tent damn it) during rest times I went out and was immediately taken by the event and the whole atmosphere and organisation that went with it. I repeated the task next year at Muirfield, this time being allocated to a scoreboard AND watching the golf in the free time. Since then I've attended just about all Opens held in Scotland. Whilst as a veteran of many campaigns now I normally go to a practice day then ensconce myself in front of the telly for the four days of the competition, I'd thoroughly recommend anyone who hasn't yet been to attend one, especially on the final day. Although you don't get to see as much golf as you'd like, the applause as the gladiators come down the eighteenth is phenomenal and there is no other atmosphere like it. The great thing too is that golfers of all nationalities get the same applause. You may have your favourite, but if your man is beaten by better golf from someone else, you applaud it, and you mean it. That's just one of the great things about golf. In football , even if it's a great game, if your team gets beat you go home disappointed – in golf you just go to witness and experience and enjoy the whole event. If the Open is my favourite week and I've now seen over 40 of them either being physically there or just watching on the telly, my favourite moment comes at the end with the phrase "And the Champion golfer of the year is…..". It still gives me goosebumps after all this time. Brilliant. And then I can't wait till next year comes around.

And still on Muirfield, I attended on the Saturday back during the 1987 Open when the weather was at its absolute worst. It takes a lot to send me home early from a golf course, but I returned home at one o'clock, a very cold and very drowned rat, but not before seeing Sandy Lyle shoot 71 in what I consider to be the finest round of golf I've ever seen. I had the pleasure of playing Muirfield two years ago with the Hamiltons and Andy M, and contrary to the public perception of many found it a very welcoming place, from both members and staff alike. Maybe it's a bit naïve of me , but is it so terrible that it wants to remain a men's club ? There are women's only clubs after all. Just a thought. I'm not sure that its discrimination as much as a few guys who just want to play in each other's company. I guess it would be different if all clubs did this and golf in general was discriminatory, but it isn't. But then again, probably I'm a bit naïve. Oh , and don't tell my mixed foursomes partner Gerri Cragg I said that. If I thought the abuse that I get when I put our ball in a bunker was bad......

One of my favourite Open memories was at Turnberry in 2009 when I attended the Wednesday practice day and watched Tom Watson, one of my favourite golfers, play a few holes. What a joy to watch and what a lesson he gave that week. He'd hit shots to the front and the back of the green, getting his distances, whereas others would just play to where the flag was. He was in superb form all week, and with no disrespect to Stewart Cink, who won that year, just about everybody in the crowd was willing him on to win at the age of 59. He came up just short, to the disappointment of many. To be fair to Stewart, for my money he had "paid his dues" as he was and is a regular visitor to the Open, something we like to see from our top golfers.

Professional golfers are often interviewed and asked what their favourite major is. Some will say the Masters, with all its splendour and played every year on the beautiful setting that is Augusta. Even my wife, who doesn't like golf will watch, albeit briefly, every April, just to see the Azaleas, the Dogwood, the assorted other flowers and the perfect green grass . It denotes the start of spring and the golfing season in the UK. American players when interviewed prior to the U.S. Open will say that is their favourite major, and try to justify it by saying any person will hold their own Open to be the best. Practically no one says the USPGA, except perhaps those who have previously won it. Whoever says any of the three above are kidding themselves. The Open is undoubtedly the original and best, with its history, its seaside courses which are miles away from big towns and a truly international field of the world's top golfers tested by the vagaries of the weather and the odd bad bounce where the ball comes to rest in the wee pot bunkers . Try hitting the ball 200 yards out of one of those babies Mr . U.S. Based Golf Pro! I love the history of it – a small event, hosting just eight golfers in the small backwater that is Prestwick back in 1860 becoming one of the world's great sporting events.

You just can't beat it.

Chapter 9

Away Days

Speaking of Turnberry, the Ailsa course there is my favourite destination to go play golf. Don't get me wrong, Milngavie is a terrific place to play , but it is good every now and again to experience a round of golf elsewhere, usually in the company of good friends such as John and David Hamilton and Andy Murrison. There are many great venues to play in Scotland, and whilst Turnberry is my favourite course, my favourite golfing memory of an away day is not from there, but came from a visit to Royal Dornoch, in the North East of Scotland. At the time I was training to be a Chartered Accountant and our company had an annual audit to do of the Royal Hotel in Ullapool. One of the managers , Gordon Rodger took on the lead role, which I thought was a bit strange , as he usually just reviewed files prepared by audit seniors and didn't travel out to do the dirty work himself. I soon found out why he had taken on the task , as before we set off to Ullapool which is situated in the North West of Scotland he said "Brian this is a five day job. What about we work at nights to finish the job early and cut across country on the

Friday and go play Dornoch?" I needed no second invitation, and sure enough we finished on the Thursday night and on Friday morning travelled over to Dornoch, a trip of some 60 miles. As we reached Dornoch it was a beautiful sunny morning with not a breath of wind, although it was frosty (it was at the beginning of April after all). As we stepped on to the tee, you could see the sun gently disperse the frost, becoming merely a glistening dew and we drove off in perfect conditions. The course itself, and the day as a whole, were just magnificent. Miles of yellow broom lines the course on one side , with the sea and the sandy beach on the other. Gordon was Club Champion at Turnberry, and playing as well as I was that year (1983, my peak so far) I challenged him off scratch – mano a mano – no strokes given or taken – real man's golf. I played well, and coming down the last we were all square. We reached the 18th green , all level, matched stroke for stroke. He was faced with a twenty foot putt, me with a twenty five foot putt. I stroked mine nicely, but to no avail, it just missing on the left hand side . Gordon, like the champion that he was, stroked his in for a one up win.

If that game is my favourite away day memory, my first memories of away days came shortly after joining the Lethamhill Sunday club. Twice a year they would go for a day out, 36 holes at courses such as Troon, Ayr Bellisle, Carnwarth and anywhere else that would take thirty golfers for two rounds on a Sunday. These were real highlights of the golfing year, although not without their own wee disasters. I remember playing at Bathgate as a thirteen year old and at the 134 yards par 3 seventeenth, with a decent score going, playing a four wood just short of the burn that guarded the green. The pin was cut just over the burn and in my efforts to be just too neat I recall chunking it into the burn four times, then getting it up and down for an eleven. Disaster ! However, I am made of stern stuff. In the afternoon round I hit my four wood to just three feet from the hole. My playing partners congratulated me for getting my revenge on the hole. I missed my putt. Golf is like that.

On yet another occasion, a friend of mine, Philip Brannan, and two friends of my brother, Frank Geary (who some years later would go on to be club Captain at Windyhill, a neighbouring course of Milngavie) and Frank Reid travelled over to Dougalston, a newly opened course in the mid seventies. We had never played such a tough course. Ribbon like fairways, trees either side, gorse and tall grass (bundai as it's commonly known) underneath the trees. A real killer. Things were going badly in terms of lost balls (although to be fair we also found a few) when we arrived at a par 3 of some 200 yards with a large pond on the left hand side. Frank G selected a five iron and hit the biggest hook I've ever seen, clearing the pond, clearing the bundai and zooming over a dilapidated house until finally crashing into some undergrowth that had been imported from the Amazon jungle. I'm sure I saw three crocodiles and David Attenborough take flight as it landed. Frank , with a straight face and without missing a beat, turned round and asked "Do you think I should play a provisional?" as we collapsed , helpless with laughter. For the non golfer, you play a provisional if you think your ball may be lost. Might have been lost? The proverbial Lord Lucan riding Shergar in the Brigadoon Steeplechase would have been easier to find. Happy days.

Yet another trip involving Andy Murrison, John and David Hamilton and myself saw us visit Machrihanish, a course with spectacular views of the Mull of Kintyre. The first at Machrihanish is a fantastic hole and it has a plaque with a quote from Jack Nicklaus "The best opening hole in the world". I'm not going to argue with Jack on that one, apparently he knows a thing or two about golf. It is a magnificent setting , a bay carved out by the Atlantic Ocean on the left hand side, and off the back tees you have a choice of how much of the bay to cut off. It's a long par 4, at 444 yards, so the more you can cut off the better. John hit his tee shot first, and being the bold man that he is announced that he was going for it. If he meant he was going for the ocean then it was a good shot, as the ball hooked off the tee and set off down the beach. I was next up and was certainly up for the task, choosing the Tiger line and like John, hooking my shot onto the beach, my pleas for relief from the casual water falling on deaf ears. David , up next, naturally took a safer route, hitting it so far right he probably still had 444 yards to go, albeit from a different direction. Andy, being the best of the four of us, creamed a drive right down the ideal line and onto the centre of the fairway. John never did find his ball, probably being washed away and ending up on the East Coast of America somewhere, thus winning the day's Long Drive contest. David, as a reward for his safe play from the tee played up the hole steadily, whilst I fortunately found my ball on the beach between puddles left by the retreating ocean. A hybrid back on track to within 90 yards of the green followed by a solid three quarter wedge and twelve foot putt secured my four, much to the chagrin of Andy, who followed his excellent drive with another excellent 3 wood which bounced just short of the green, bounced slightly right, and got lost in the bundai. Such is golf, there just ain't no justice. Despite it being in February, we had bright sunshine all day and we have photos of us in short sleeves going up the 18th (albeit the jumpers were immediately on after the photoshoot !). A great day, and well worth the visit. A word of praise for my playing companions – John the great enthusiast, David, who apart from having a tidy golf game is a great amateur photographer, and normally takes excellent photos of the surrounding scenery (I've got two of his shots at Gleneagles blown up and hanging on my wall) and Andy, who comfortably plays off the magic five, providing most of the real golf played and doesn't seem to mind on the odd occasion when I outdrive him being chided for being a duffer. Great guys who share my love of the history of the game and play it in a great spirit.

I've had many, many (too many as my wife will tell you) brilliant away days at golf, and I always look forward to the next one. Like the Open, you just canny beat it.

Just for the record, here's my top ten of courses for away days (good if you can get a deal, some can be expensive!) There may be better courses, but if there are, I haven't played them yet. Ask me again in five years time, after I've played a few more on my wish list. My rankings by then may well be different, but they'll take some beating. If anyone wants to invite me to Augusta, Pebble Beach, Royal Portrush, Royal Melbourne or any other such course in an effort to get on the list, I'd just like to say I'm open to offers.

1. Turnberry Ailsa
2. Royal Dornoch
3. Old Course, St. Andrew's
4. Royal County Down
5. Muirfield
6. King's Course, Gleneagles
7. Dundonald
8. Carnoustie
9. Kingsbarnes
10. Spey Valley

Chapter 10

The Tools of the Trade

My first set of clubs was your typical half set in one respect. Typical in that it consisted of a driver, a three, five, seven, nine iron and putter. That's where any sense of "typicalness", if that's a word, ends. In the most sense, my half set displayed….. well, let's just call it character. A ten year old being presented with this amalgam of clubs today would turn their nose up and refuse to touch them. It was not your nice matched , made to suit junior half set. Every club was a different make, every one cut down to my size, so I suppose in a way it was a sort of made to measure set. I loved my driver. A nice brown wooden head, grey steel shaft, rubber grip fitted. I could crack that driver 100 yards down the middle , every time. Without a word of a lie, my stats on fairways hit would have beaten the number one driver on the USPGA tour. Two hundred yards shorter, admittedly, but hey I was only ten, and a very small ten at that. I didn't use my three iron a lot. The face had a dimpled pattern and it had a wooden shaft cut down to my size. The leather grip had been unwound from the original top of the shaft and put back in place in a professional manner, but it was not a great favourite. The five iron looked suspiciously like a Glasgow Parks five iron but again cut down to size, with blue tape at the bottom of the rubber grip. The seven iron, my favourite iron had a brown steel shaft (obviously one of the first steel shafts, to make it look like wood). I used it from 50 yards and in, consigning my nine iron, which looked like the cousin of my three iron but with grooves instead of dimples, to my bag, only to be used on the very odd emergency occasion or when in a bunker. My putter was a work of art, a hickory shafted blade putter with a slightly off set head. It had a lovely leather grip, which alas was prone to coming loose. It was held up by black masking tape, which was renewed on a regular basis. In the early days it was a lethal weapon, but as I grew bigger it felt too light and I asked my dad to put a bit of weight on it . My dad was many things , but he was not a welder, so he gave it to Big Rab Harper our next door neighbour, who may well have had some idea of welding, but no idea of golf obviously. Instead of a nice rectangle strip of lead that I had anticipated, neatly aligned on the club head, Rab welded a huge daud (piece) of rusty metal onto the back of it. Don't get me wrong – I was grateful that he gave it a go, but I wish I had been more specific about my instructions, a lesson I guess I've never really learned since then. I still have that putter, and some twenty years after the weld went on, I had the big lump of metal removed. Alas, the markings on the back of the putter came off with the rusty daud. I'd love to know just who made that old putter, but I just can't remember the maker's name, and I guess I'll never know. I occasionally dig the putter out of the cupboard and knock a few putts off a glass, just for old times sake.

These days , being a proper golfer, I would not be seen with anything less than a nearly new Pro V1 on my tee (during the season at any rate). In those days I would use anything that was nearly round that I could get my hands on. Price's Everlasting, which were exactly that, a solid lump of rubber. The occasional forty year old ball with the funny inverted dimples, which I now wished I had kept . The Penfold Ace, which looked shiny and brand new, except when you turned it round it revealed a huge smile on its face, the slash caused no doubt by an almighty thin shot with a lethally bladed sand iron. But to me it was kind of nearly round, so it was used nonetheless. Now and then you would find a Dunlop 65, which some good golfer , who obviously had a well paid job , had lost in the rough. I'm probably wrong, but my recollection of the ball in those days was that they felt denser than those we use today. The ball these days undoubtedly goes a lot further, but in the old days they were the smaller (1.62inch as opposed to 1.68 inch) and the more dense balls were less likely to be bumped off line when putting ? Or was it just that I was a better putter then ? Or that my misty memory just remembers that things were better in the old days ?

Since my early days ,and going back to clubs, like many golfers I've had many sets of clubs. My second set was when I inherited my brother's mixed set. I didn't really take to them, but it was a full set of clubs. I remember a nice wooden headed two wood with a bone like insert in its face and it having a slight bend in the shaft near the head. The binding connecting the head to the shaft was forever coming loose and required constant rewinding and tying. The irons were a bit of a mishmash, although at least they all had steel shafts. It was with some joy therefore when for Christmas 1973, my parents got me a new set of McGregor Tourney irons, and a couple of new woods, and at 14 years of age I looked the business. Bizarrely, it would be some forty years before I would get my next new set of irons. At 18 years of age I swapped my McGregor Tourneys with John McDowall for a set of Lynx irons. These lasted a good while until (in desperation at some more poor form I have to say) I bought a second hand set of Tiger Shark clubs. A bit odd shaped, but I had bought into some publicity in a magazine about them being "game improvers". Big mistake, and I soon bought a second hand set of Ping irons (good choice), followed by a second hand set of Callaway X14's (excellent clubs), then Callaway x 20 tour (ebay purchase, shafts too stiff, ¾ of an inch too small, not mentioned in the advertising blurb) until I finally thought that at age fifty plus, and with the kids now in gainful employment, I'd treat myself to new custom fit irons. A shiny new set of Titleist AP2s, and lovely they are too. Went the whole hog and got a Titleist 913D3 driver as well. No excuses for poor play now, and just at the right time, as I approach my golfing peak.

My set is now complete with a Callaway 3 wood and Ping 5 wood, both of which I've had for some time, and a newly acquired Odyssey number nine, the putter that Phil won the Masters with a few years ago. I've tended to favour mallet headed putters over the years, interspersed with the occasional Scotty Cameron , Ping Anser , Ping Kushin, Ping B60, Wilson 832, etc, etc as I sought the putter that would be the equal of that first wooden shafted putter of 45 years ago. I've visited golf shops, junk shops, antique shops in the knowledge that there is an old wooden hickory shafted putter out there somewhere that is the "one". The one that was made especially for my hands, and the one that will help me to win the Open. But , sad to say, and Bono of U2 probably puts this best, when he named a song after my search "I still haven't found what I'm looking for", and I guess I never will. I am pleased to report however, that Phil's Odyssey number nine is showing great signs of being the modern equivalent of "the one". My search for that perfect wooden shafted putter, though it will go on forever, now has a less frantic note to it.

And a quick word about golfing attire. Critics of the game will take great pleasure in ridiculing a sport whose standard mode of dress is akin to a colour blind Chicago pimp of the 1970's but I have never subscribed to the garish threads that the professionals in the game seem to wear. Labels have never been a big issue for me, except that my jumpers have to be quality – Pringle in the old days, Glenmuir now that you can't seem to get Pringle jerseys except in incredibly high priced fashion shops. Oh and Footjoy shoes. Got to have those. Have tried others, but keep coming back to them. Those who know me will perhaps point out that despite me claiming to be conservatively dressed, I now adorn some natty headgear, having worn a trilby for the last two years or so. This , I find, has earned me some new found respect, and other golfers do take note. I think that this is because it truly makes a fashion statement….probably along the lines of "Here is a middle aged twat trying to look cool and failing miserably". But, a fashion statement nonetheless, and hey, it does make me stand out from the crowd, and as someone once said, "Ain't no such thing as bad publicity!"

Chapter 11

Would You Believe It ?

The first question that a non golfer will ask a golfer is "have you ever had a hole in one ?". In my view a hole in one is very overrated. What one golfer who has been fortunate enough to have had one might describe as "the perfect shot", his partner would describe as "the luckiest shot I've ever seen". And apart from all that, golfing tradition dictates that you buy everyone in the clubhouse a drink, so what's so good about that? There is a story about a famous local golfer, Charlie Green , holing out in one and asking his playing companions if they had seen where his ball went (he was playing into a strong sun). On hearing the reply "No, sorry Charlie", Charlie then played a provisional, declared the first one lost and then feigned surprise when they found his original in the hole. Charlie obviously agreed with my sentiments. At this point the reader will probably think I'm saying this just because I haven't had one. But that's not true. The truth of the matter is that I don't know whether I've had one or not.

To the logically minded, this statement doesn't make much sense. You've either had one or you've not . Can't be simpler than that. Well let me explain. I was fifteen years of age and playing the twelfth hole at Lethamhill, a par 3 which plays 150 yards uphill. Playing off the front tees with a gentle breeze at my back, I played a lovely seven iron up the hill , over the bunker towards the flag. "Very tidy" I thought, "that'll be close". As I strode up the hill towards the green I was greeted by three small boys who asked "Who played that great shot Mister ?" . As I was playing alone I would've thought that was fairly obvious, but I asked them what great shot were they talking about. "The great shot that went right into the hole there" they said. And sure enough, when I went over to the flag, there lay the ball, securely resting at the bottom of the cup. To this day I don't know whether or not I did achieve that elusive hole in one, or whether it was kicked into the hole by one of the three "outside agencies".

I've come close since then, but as the saying goes, no cigar. My most recent near miss came at the Open at Muirfield in 2013. You may not have seen it on the telly, but HSBC were running a nearest the pin competition on a golf simulator in the tented village. The hole was the 13th at Muirfield I think, and I watched a dozen or so competitors who were in front of me in the queue. They all seemed to be going short right. Come my turn, I requested a six iron, hit it well, and came up short right. Using a bit of savvy, I asked for a five iron aimed a bit left and hit my second shot pin high, but just right. For my final effort I aimed a bit more left and the ball bounced on the green ran up to the hole and at the last minute veered right, finishing up just 1 foot 10 inches away. As it turned out I did indeed finish nearest the pin that day, and received a Muirfield 18th hole flag signed by Like Donald. There was a bigger prize for the nearest to the pin for the whole of that week, but I didn't win it. Some hacker probably fluked a lucky hole in one , no doubt.

But though I had little luck on that occasion, luck did play a part in my biggest win at golf to date. A few years back, that man John Hamilton had organised a summer eclectic competition. For those unfamiliar with the event , you record your best score at each hole throughout the season, deduct half your handicap, and the winner is the person with the lowest net score. Sixteen of us had entered , at twenty quid a head, winner takes all. With one round to go I was 1.5 strokes ahead of Andy Murrison and Raymond Vezza , another dawn patrol veteran. As I prepared to tee off mid afternoon, Raymond had just finished his round and gleefully proclaimed that he had birdied two of the holes he previously only had par on, so he was the new leader. Was he winding me up ? Whilst I pondered this and stepped on to the first tee, Andy Murrison ,who also plays early morning, putted out on the eighteenth green, giving a Tiger fist pump as his putt went in. As Andy is normally a fairly unemotional character, being a member of the banking community, it didn't take a genius to work out that he had improved his score by at least two shots, so whether Raymond had been bluffing or not (he wasn't as it turned out), the pressure was indeed well and truly on. What added to the pressure was that I only had four realistic chances to improve my score, needing a birdie at either the fourth (take that one away – I can't get within 60 yards of it in two), the sixth, the ninth, the eleventh or the fifteenth to win. The fourth hole passed , predictably, without a birdie being threatened. The sixth is a short par three of only 133 yards, downhill. It's a hole that most people will birdie at least once in the season, but somewhat frustratingly for me at that point, not me. The flag was at the back of the green and I hit an aggressive shot, right down the flag. The ball bounced three feet short of the stick, took a small hop then ran a further twelve feet…..and with the last roll , trickled down the bank and through the green. Curses ! I was left with a very delicate shot which I played beautifully , a small lob which landed just on the green, rolled straight towards the hole, and then broke sharply left, agonisingly lipping out at the last minute. Two down, three to go.

It was then that Lady Luck smiled on me. The ninth is a difficult par 4 of 374 yards, but plays longer than that and has a blind drive. It was into a slight breeze that day, and as I hadn't looked at a birdie there all season, the omens weren't good. When I hit a less than perfect drive, slightly left onto a downhill lie, with some 170 yards to the flag, the chances didn't look good on this occasion either. Wanting to be up to give myself an opportunity, I selected a four iron for my second shot, which although decently struck was smothered a bit left, not travelling any higher than three feet off the ground. Had the ball not struck the yellow post denoting the bridge over the burn some 60 yards short of the green, my ball would've finished pin high thirty yards left of the green with a devil of a pitch over a bunker to get to the flag. A par, never mind a birdie would have been out of the question. But the ball did hit that yellow post, leapt 30 foot into the air, ricocheting hard right at an angle of forty five degrees and finished on the front of the green , thirty foot short of the flag. "This has birdie written all over it!" I smiled to my playing companions. And indeed it did. My thirty footer was all uphill, and I gave it a smash with my putter, the ball hit the back of the hole, jumped six inches in the air, and plopped back down into the bottom of the cup. A winning birdie ! I could and should have birdied the eleventh (which would have taken the pressure off because I still didn't know how many birdies Andy Murrison had) but at the end up it didn't matter, he only had the two as it turned out. Lady Luck had indeed smiled upon me. I still have the ball, complete with yellow paint mark on it, to remind me good things still happen on golf courses. Sometimes you need it.

To be fair to myself, I did give Lady Luck a hand by displaying some measure of determination during the event. Some weeks before, whilst leading, I had injured my wrist (alas not in some manly rugby type injury or something of that ilk, but a Chartered Accountant type injury – I wasn't holding my mouse for the computer correctly) and should have given it a rest. But I was in contention, so I was definitely giving it a go…..even though, because of lack of wrist cock, I was only hitting it 160 yards or so. However, I reckoned there were four par threes that I could maybe birdie, so I went out, and at the par 3 twelfth, a hole of 174 yards downhill, I hit a driver (normally a six iron) to 20 feet and holed the putt for a two. In a strange twist of fate I got a double benefit from that round – my handicap went up from 9 to 10 that day – adding a 0.1 to make 9.5 , and thus I got an half extra shot to deduct from my ultimate score!

I did intend to spend that £320 on some new golf gear, but as ever, it went into the household budget and was frittered away on non essentials such as food and rent. No matter, the whole thing had a "would you believe it" aspect about it, which still makes me smile. Can't say the same for Raymond and Andy though……

Definitely a candidate for "Would You Believe It" is Cameron Watson, who happens to be the General Manager at the company I work for, and regularly robs people of their cash due to his improbably high handicap. (I'm sure he gives a percentage of his winnings to the Match and Handicap Committee at Airdrie Golf Club, but that's another story). Anyway, we were playing in a charity event down in Wales, and after 9 holes we were congratulating ourselves on playing reasonably well and remarking on how pleasant the day was . Those familiar with golf will know that this is signal to the Golfing Gods, and sure enough, as we stood on the tenth tee it began to rain. Now, having lived in the West of Scotland for fifty odd years, I'm well used to copious amounts of rain. Let me tell you, Scotland is strictly second division compared to the amount of water that can fall in a short time in Wales (think Ryder Cup at Celtic Manor). By the time we got to the tenth green we were soaked through, and Cameron's game started to deteriorate. Fast forward to the 18th and he had hardly contributed to the team score on the back nine. So, when he reached the rain sodden bunker in three, some 90 yards short of the green, I'm thinking maybe he should just pick up and seek sanctuary of the clubhouse. But no.

To my, and our playing partner Andy Oxley's surprise he marched into the bunker, armed with a fairway wood. "Good Lord , no!" I thought, and one look at Andy's face told me he was thinking the same. "The constant rain dripping on his head has been like an hour and a half of the Chinese Water torture treatment– he's clearly gone insane" . Quickly followed by "When he's played this, will you or I go help him dig the ball out of the face of the bunker?" Our thoughts were interrupted as Cameron swiped at the ball which then cleared the lip, took two bounces on the swimming pool that was masquerading as a green and stopped two feet from the hole, for a tap in 5 net 4 and two points. I'd love to say that shot, which Seve in his prime would've been proud of won us the competition, but it didn't. To this day however, I'm still not sure I believe it. I saw it but I'm not sure I believe it. It does illustrate however that old golfing mantra – to play a shot you have to see it in your mind, and if you can see it in your mind you can play it. Cameron obviously had seen it, though I still think his temporary insanity played a major part in it.

Chapter 12

Home on the Range

I have to confess that I just like hitting golf balls. There's something quite therapeutic about smashing golf balls into the ether, time after time after time. So it will come as no surprise that it's quite common to find me on the Golf Range at World of Golf in Drumchapel, which is thankfully strategically placed just two minutes from my house. This is particularly true in the winter months when there is no possibility of proper play at night or when it's peeing it down at the weekend. Now, I realise that not all golfers think this way. A big part of the attraction of golf is wandering around a nicely prepared field in the company of friends, and meeting the challenges that each hole and indeed each different shot presents. The golf range does not have these advantages, and banging away for frustrating hours on end trying to achieve golfing perfection can be unattractive to some. More than that, golf ranges can indeed be hazardous places to be. For a start, the mats that you hit from can be quite unforgiving and damaged tendons can be the result of thump after thump of golf club connecting with the solid base that is the composition of the mat. On a cold winter's night, a slightly thinned shot can cause a painful tingling in the fingers, despite the best intentions and design of the new easy to hit cavity back irons. To be fair, being a man of some aspiration to be a serious golfer (aka poseur) , my clubs are slightly less forgiving than most, and I can tell you I've paid for it with a few less than clean hits which normally invokes the phrase " Ah ya bas….." before realising you're in the company of children and adults alike , and you just stop short of venting your real feelings.

But there are many other distractions which can put the non addict off going to the range. By its nature, the range attracts people who are just starting off in golf. They can bash away to their hearts content, not having to look for their ball in the rough or the trees and importantly not holding anyone up either. There is a danger in this however. A golf club and a golf ball combo can be lethal weapons, from any distance or angle, and many a time I've been on the range, about to pull the trigger on yet another glorious iron that will send the ball soaring into the night sky when "crack!" and I nearly shit myself as the guy in the next bay toes one off the end of the club, the ball clattering into the thin board separating him from me. Equally effective is the one that he or she skies , the ball jettisoning off the iron roof above with a noise that would indeed waken the dead and rebounding back into the bays, sending everyone diving for cover. Believe me, after either of those shots, the next dozen or so of your balls are played with a nervous tick. Concentration is impossible when you know the next misguided missile could be coming your way from next door at any time. And just when he or she has hit a few decent ones, and you start to settle down.........

But the hazards of the range are not just confined to the novice. Hell no. There are much worse agonies in store for the regular range goer. None is more dangerous to your health than the more advanced golfer who has purchased a new driver. Having just purchased the new super hit-it-further – than Bubba Watson driver , he'll smash it drive after drive , the impact emitting a high pitched screech each time, thanks to the uber new technology thin faced titanium driver. Ear shattering emissions are guaranteed time after time and you know you've timed your entrance to coincide with him just starting on the third of his one hundred and twenty balls he's purchased. And every single one to be hit with his new baby. Come to think of it, a new baby's whining would be infinitely more pleasurable.

However, the sound of this tinny ear piercing agony is nothing compared to the agony of listening to "the coach". The coach is usually a twenty something handicap player who knows everything about the golf swing and feels the need to impart his knowledge to his buddy on each and every shot. The poor victim of the coach will normally end up a frustrated and confused wreck , knowing the coach will take the credit for the one good one he hit out of the bucket of a hundred. The other ninety nine bad ones, were of course, down to the player himself. For those who accuse me of occasionally being "the coach", in my defence at least I know what I'm talking about, not like those other guys. In the same category of people we don't want to hear is the "I'm a businessman and I'm going to tell my friend, who I've not seen for a few years (and indeed the whole of the range) about my business affairs in a very loud voice indeed" man. We're really not interested in your dealings with the VAT man or how that big sales order that you were counting on was cancelled, so if you want to bore your long lost friend, take him for a coffee, and leave us alone to hit our balls in peace please.

Oh and one last tip. Do not under any circumstances play from the bay next to a long hitter. Even if all the other bays are full, wait until another one becomes free. If you do not heed my advice and decide to go ahead, you will ultimately not only feel wholly inadequate but will ruin your own swing at the same time . This applies to men only, who by nature will attempt to compete in a macho show of foolishness, and inevitably end up failing miserably . On the other hand, ladies , with their inbuilt capacity for common sense, tend to have a more realistic view of things and play within their own capabilities. They can ignore this last piece of sage counsel.

Golf ranges have improved enormously over the years. The one I use, World of Golf at Drumchapel , is top notch. Bays upstairs and downstairs. A coffee shop/bistro forms part of the complex. An American Golf shop with all the gear is attached. There's a gym where you can hear the young guns pumping vast quantities of iron, which to be fair, I could do as well....if

I'd the use of a fork lift that is. Nice new golf balls. Pop up tees. And modern technology. The latest in trackman equipment to help your game. A young attendant tried to sell the concept to me. Twenty five quid he said, and you can monitor your swing angle, your swing speed, spin rate, dispertion, club angle , degrees of how open or closed the clubface is at impact. What you do is play your shots and then compare your stats to the tour pros – give it a go free for ten minutes he said. "What's your handicap?" he asked. "Eight" I replied. "Well at your level, let's look at your swing speed first. Hit a few drives and we'll match it against the pros", he said brightly. Under his watchful eye, I hit half a dozen shots, and he looked at the readings. "Of course" he said, scratching his chin and looking slightly concerned, as if he was struggling for the right words , "of course, we measure decent amateurs like you against the ladies pros….they hit it a long way these days". Twenty five quid to be told I hit the ball like a big girl ? No sale. See macho comments above.

Yet, despite these hazards, I can thoroughly recommend that you use the golf range to practice. Yes, it's not nearly as good as the real thing , but it gets you out the house, honing your swing and even if it doesn't quite perfect it, you're still hitting golf balls. And that's got to be good, hasn't it ?

Chapter 13

The Milngavie Players

For those unfamiliar with Milngavie (pronounced Mil-guy) it is, without doubt, one of the more affluent areas around Glasgow. When I joined Milngavie Golf Club in 1986 I was told by friends that it might be difficult to fit in with those posh types. By nature, I'm not a worrier of things like that, but if I had been, I would have been worrying unnecessarily. Yes, there were some who exhibited a "superiority complex", and not in a golfing sense, but in the main I've found the people friendly and good to play golf with. And there have certainly been an entertaining mix of people's company to enjoy over the last 28 years. Take the boys from the Thomson McCrone team , who won the 2013 competition with a perfect 9 wins out of 9. How they managed to win the semi final and final without me after I got my handicap cut and thus played my way out of the side I'll never know (though skip Eddie McLeod reckoned that was indeed the reason they won them). But they are great company and we had great times. My colleagues from the Jessiman team from earlier years – perennial underachievers given their vast ability, a team of golfing greats who inexplicably and with alarming frequency , tend to make first round exits. In one of my last games for them, my partner Paul Geoghan and I were 3 down with 3 to play. Having home advantage, we reckoned that if we could get three pars to finish we could make a difference (all 18 holes count in the Jessiman format) . We did, and we did......finishing 6 down as our lame pars were outdone by our opponents who birdied 16,17 and 18. Much abuse followed from our team mates and deservedly so. But great fun nonetheless.

Individuals come to mind – for example, my friend and playing partner for a number of years Rodger Shirley. If you mention any part of the world, Rodger will have been there and will be able to tell you tales of the copious amounts of random people he has met throughout the globe. Dougie Kirkham , a past captain who regularly wins the annual Milngavie Worzel Gummidge look alike contest, and had the brass neck to tell a junior off for not having his shirt tucked in. Graeme Jolly, a taxi driver whose business is always quiet and is only able to go on six holidays a year as a result. Poor soul. And past member Alan Little, who responded to my cheery first greeting of "How ye doing ?" with the classic response of "They've just sent me here to die". A coupon buster of a reply if ever there was one. It turned out Alan had major health problems, including a fight with cancer. I'm sure he won't mind me saying that he was a bit of a rogue when he was younger, but he loved his golf and he and I became firm friends, teaming up to win the Winter League one year, unbeaten in 12 games. He is a fighter, and I remember him playing a final with cracked ribs (would've been better playing with golf clubs I suppose) and ultimately winning at the twenty first hole. Unfortunately he left Milngavie, having suggested that a past captain was a vertically challenged person of questionable parentage , following a major difference of opinion. Like all families, and I like to think of Milngavie as a family club , life isn't always perfect and like everyone else it has its problems, but there really is no finer place to be.

There have been many other characters and fine people I've met at Milngavie, but maybe Anna Telfer deserves a special mention. Back in 2007, Anna became the first woman to become Captain and what a difference she made.

Most Captains like to make their mark by adding something to the club that stands the test of time. Andrew McGarvie, a previous Captain had a stone shelter constructed at our fourteenth hole. "McGarvie's Folly" it was called due to its apparently high cost, but it has stood the test of time and many have sheltered there in extreme weather. Robin O'Neill had a new practice short game area constructed with two USPGA spec greens built. As you can imagine , this didn't come cheap. "O'Neill's Folly" it was called, but used and appreciated by many. Anna not to be outdone, splashed out twenty five quid and introduced Tidy Tees to Milngavie Golf Club. A significant development within the golf club, and are still on our tees to this day, though largely ignored by the many. In all seriousness however, Anna ran the club well that year and did an exceptionally fine job. She is also a member of the ladies all conquering Greenlees team which seem to sweep all before them year after year. It is also to be pointed out , before MGC is accused of having a token lady as Captain, that more ladies have been asked to become Captain since then, but have shown a great deal of common sense by turning the post down . In my view the job has become more difficult in recent years, given the declining number of people wishing to become members, with waiting lists a thing of the past. New and fresh challenges seem to present themselves year on year and it takes a special commitment to take on the role these days.

One such man who also deserves acclaim is the previously mentioned and much maligned Dougie Kirkham, who was an exceptional captain back in 2005. What made him exceptional was not his fantastic administration or diplomatic skills but the suspicion that he was the first Celtic supporting Captain at Milngavie in over one hundred years of Milngavie Golf Club. When I joined back in 1986 the club had a wee bit of a reputation for having members who supported a football team from the South Side of the City. Since then, MGC has obviously gone downhill, allowing Dougie and many other Celtic supporters to join the ranks. But that's progress for you, and the banter is all the better for it.

It would be remiss of me not to give that bad man John Hamilton another mention. He was Captain in 2006, and if he ruined my game by persuading me to become Junior Convenor I like to think I got my revenge. Sometime around

2009, and on the same 15th hole at Milngavie where he committed the heinous crime of getting me to agree to be on the committee, I noticed that he was playing with a Winfield ball. This type of ball was one of the cheapest on the market when they stopped producing them twenty years before, and with no disrespect to the brand, they were not frequently used by top golfers. Allied to this I noted that he was playing with a set of his dad's ancient Fazer clubs, which were some thirty years old and in extremely poor condition. Indeed, the year before , I remember his sand wedge split, sending a chard of metal through his finger, only being removed after a painful operation. Well I gave him dog's abuse. "How can you", I opined, " a past Captain of Milngavie Golf Club, disgrace the club by using such old and unfashionable equipment? No wonder your handicap has gone up from 6 to 9 over the last 3 years !". Our playing companions, Andy Murrison and David Hamilton joined in the fun, and John was left in no doubt that to continue to play in high company such as ours he would have to bring his equipment up to date.

He took this warning to heart, and two weeks later he would turn up on the tee with a brand new set of custom fitted Taylor Made, complete with shiny new Taylor made golf balls. Five years on from that conversation his golf has worsened considerably and he now plays off a handicap of 15. I like to think that I've been instrumental in his decline, revenge for his wickedness of all those years ago. Thankfully he is now in the process of reversing his poor run of form, and I'm sure it won't be long before he is knocking on the door of single figures again , though this year he has a new grand daughter to contend with, potentially a draw on time even worse than being on the committee.......

And it would be also remiss of me not to mention Lindsay Renfrew, a legend at Milngavie. Honorary President, Past Captain, Scottish Amateur Internationalist, winner of the club championship umpteen times, now well over eighty years of age but still able to play to an eleven handicap. And still with perfect eyesight, as he proved by commenting favourably (from a distance of a short par 4 away) on the nineteen year old ladies club champion who was wearing tight shorts at the time....

I could probably write a whole book just on the people I've met at Milngavie Golf Club, from the "Four Commancheros" of Gordon Bell/John Bryan/John McKerracher/Herbie Fellowes of the world who ensure there's always laughter around the clubhouse to the clubmaster Hugh Park who will always ensure there's some argument around, to the secretary Susan Woods, who is well short of retirement age but has been at Milngavie at least a hundred years to keep things in order, but that would take too long, and I know there's a couple of sharp lawyers who may take interest, and I don't want sued ! Safe to say I'd like to thank each and every one of them for the good times I've enjoyed in their company at MGC.

Chapter 14

Not Quite Bruce

For me , golf has always been an entertaining game. Not just for the game itself, although it's ever changing challenges entertains on its own, but through the chat and the banter that pervades through the sport. Admittedly, much of it can be adolescent in its nature (talk of stiff shafts and quips about golfers balls for example), but if you're spending four hours at a particular place , and it's not work, then by my reckoning you should get some measure of entertainment from it. These days , I am considered in some circles as an entertainer on the golf front (not quite Bruce Forsyth mind you), and am occasionally asked by the golf club to perform at social occasions such as Burns Suppers and music/comedy nights. I like to think I'm asked due to my sparkling wit, but in truth it's possibly due to the fact that I'm cheap (free). Although I've developed my material over a number of years, in a golfing sense I first started to write about golf at the age of 16. I had gone to St. Andrew's to play in a boy's tournament, and prior to playing the Eden Course where the qualifying was held, I had a game at the New and Jubilee courses. Whilst I don't remember much about my rounds on these (except I remember the New being an excellent course and the Jubilee not so good – though they've much improved that since then I believe), wandering about those two courses brought to mind a poem by Sir John Betjeman "Seaside Golf", in which he extols the virtues of golf at the seaside on a bright sunny day. Fairly obviously the weather wasn't just as kind to me, and I remember jotting down notes on the back of scorecards and golf ball wrappers in the cold and rain. A footnote for those under the age of forty – golf balls used to be individually wrapped and what a pleasure it was unwrapping a "brannie" (brand new golf ball). Sadly missed.

Anyhow, I digress. Having collected my scribbled-on scorecards and golf ball wrappers, when I got back home I put it all together and composed " The True Story Of Seaside Golf" which I'm led to believe narrowly missed out on a Booker or Purlitzer Prize or Nobel Peace Prize or something. It went :

"How low it flew, how crooked too,
It just cleared the end of the tee,

And grovelling, disappeared from view,
Bounding off a boulder, into the sea.
A terrible drive, one of my worst,
That made partners snigger, as I cursed.

So three off the tee I drove once more,
Like an arrow, true in flight,
Die straight, a gust of wind and then
It veered a sickening right.
And as I cursed this freakish weather,
I knew I'd find it in the heather.

And there it lay; buried, the most horrible of lies,
A hack, a ton of sand, the blinding of both eyes.
But then with the luckiest shot I'd ever seen ,
I topped an eight iron on to the green.
And though just three feet away, no more than four ,
Three jabs were added to my score.

What is it with this desolate place,
With hell hole bunkers hidden from view?
And driving wind and rain in face,
Fingers numbed and turning blue.
With hateful oaths that fill the air,

And seagulls droppings everywhere.

Despite the tone, in actual fact I love seaside golf. It truly is the best.

Entertainment abounds at Milngavie Golf Club when the boys from Masserene, a club in Northern Ireland come to visit every second year. Both clubs were formed in 1895, and in the centenary year a delegation was sent by the committee to negotiate an annual match between the two clubs. Masserene put up a Shillelagh as the trophy and it was decided the winner would be the aggregate holes up/down on a home and away basis. I didn't play in the first few (club Captain Brian Adair obviously recognised talent, or rather lack of it), but played in a few thereafter. As you'd expect there were a number of characters involved and I remember playing Barry and Seamus at Milngavie who were intent on giving each other as hard a time as possible. "Great Shot Barry!" Seamus would exclaim "well at least it would've been had the green been 40 yards to the left instead of that deep rough where the ball now is!!" . Barry would not be outdone. "Lovely swing Seamus, pure poetry…..more McGonnigal than Burns mind you……but poetry nonetheless" Great pals, and very good golfers, seeing my partner and I off by two holes if I remember correctly. Tragically, Seamus was killed in a motor accident, and I know he's sadly missed by all at Masserene.

Having had experience of this kind of banter, I was ready when I was asked to say a few words to greet the visitors one year. I commenced my speech with

> "Welcome to Masserene, for they are here,
> To take our women and drink our beer.
> To beat us at golf and that's no good,
> And afterwards eat all our food.
> It's nice to see them, but all the same,
> We wish they bandits would go back hame "

I think they appreciated that, given the amount of abuse and the large number of objects thrown my way !

But banter aside, like all games, they were competitive. I remember playing in thunder and lightning down 17 and 18 at Masserene, because we were three up and the Masserene boys , Alistair and Andrew wanted a chance to finish

18 only 1 down ! (they did). And I recall being in the last game at Milngavie another year, winning 3 up , but being the villain of the piece among my team mates because I had been 5 up previously and only winning 3 up allowed Masserene to square the match overall. A comprehensive winner yet a target for abuse ! Yet another golfing injustice if ever there was one !

And that's the great thing about golf. At least at the level I play at. We all want to win, yes, but in 99.9% of games I've played in it's played in the right spirit. Take my winter league partner, Ian McLeod. Ian plays off 28 and is 71 years of age. We're 5 down going up the eleventh and the wind and the rain is battering us. He can hardly see through his rain splattered glasses. But he's getting a stroke at eleven, and with a good second shot he can get up close to the green and maybe pinch a hole back. He puts his ball on the mat that we use in the winter months to protect the fairways. The wind picks up a bit more, deluging more rain upon his already soaked frame. But he carefully goes through his routine, swings at the ball, hits the mat 15 yards whilst the ball goes nowhere, like a magician doing the famous table cloth trick. He has a quick peek up to see if we are looking. We are. He takes a bow. Marvellous. Or Bruce Coburn, a Thomson McCrone colleague on the first tee of an important game. Handicaps must be sorted out, so I ask him "What are you, Bruce?" He spreads his hands upwards and outwards, "A sex God" he proclaims. And obviously prone to self delusions, but the right attitude nonetheless.

As I said , golf is an entertaining game, and one that requires great imagination. Bruce obviously has it in spades.

Chapter   15

Mano a Mano

Matchplay. The purest form of golf. That is if you believe many people, notably golf commentators, who clamour for more matchplay tournaments for the professionals. Man versus man, you against him. Head to head. Mano a mano. I'm sure its a macho thing. It's how the game first started , they say, and we should have more of it. I'm not so sure. I've got a sneaky feeling that the guys who are such enthusiasts of matchplay are guys who are not as consistent as perhaps they should be , who think that taking eight at a hole should just be wiped out as a blip and not really damage their prospects too much. There's no doubt that whilst I enjoy matchplay, and indeed there's nothing more enjoyable than a nice friendly fourball match on a lovely summers evening with nothing but pride at stake, I've always had the view that it's what you total up over eighteen holes that counts . That you've met each of the challenges presented to you by the golf course (and indeed yourself) all the way round and come through with your total, good or bad. Then you can whinge and grumble afterwards to anyone that will listen, and even those who don't….. "if it wasn't for that seven at the fourth and those two sixes at twelve and seventeen, I would've had a 68". And then to hear that quaint old Glaswegian expression from your friends " and if my Granny had whatsits she would've been ma Granda". The fact is you did get a seven and two sixes and should thus be punished accordingly. To me there's something not quite right about someone who scores seventeen fours and a ten (total 78, I'm an accountant, trust me) beating someone who scores sixteen fours and two fives (74 if you can't be bothered doing the maths). I can honestly say that I'd prefer playing one under my handicap, getting my handicap cut by 0.2 and finishing fifth in a tournament to playing a matchplay game and winning one up.

It may be strange to learn then, that my favourite week of the year in the golfing calendar at the golf club is the week of the Club Championship. This is the week, usually mid June, where the sixteen best golfers in the club compete against each other in matchplay. Yes, I know it's not strokeplay, but the thing I like about it is that the games are played off scratch, i.e. no handicap strokes given or taken. Don't get me wrong, the handicap system in golf is an excellent invention – it enables golfers of all abilities to compete against each other, but for me there's something instrinsically not quite right if I, (off a handicap of eight and receiving a deduction of eight strokes from my score) beat a scratch golfer when I shoot 74 and he shoots 70. So it's a delight for me when I occasionally qualify for the last sixteen of the club championship to play against the best players at the club. Qualifying usually means scoring well in two of three qualifying rounds and the best scratch fifteen , plus last year's winner, go head to head knockout, last 16 on Monday, quarter finals on Wednesday, semi finals on Friday then a thirty six hole final on the Sunday, when our own champion is crowned.

So how occasional is occasionally ? Well, I've played in twenty seven of these qualifiers and made it through to the last sixteen a grand total of three times. Given that my handicap has ranged from 7 to 12 in that period, that low number is not entirely surprising, though my feeling is that I should have made it through on many more occasions. One time in particular still haunts me . I had shot a well played first round of 74 which set me up nicely, and in the second round made a solid start with a par at the first. At the second, a nice downhill par three of 162 yards, I hit a good six iron to thirty feet past the hole . The putt was straight downhill, and I hit a solid putt which came up just eight inches short. Normally I would've just tapped in for a three, but I was going to be standing on my partner, Graham Bell's line, so I announced I would mark it. Graham said "don't bother its ok – on you go". " Na," I said, "I'll wait…just to be sure". " No it's ok", Graham insisted "it won't make any difference to my line". I hesitated, and then decided ok, but crucially my mind was not settled and in an effort to tap in and not stand on his line , tweaked the putt and it missed. Bogey. Out of nothing. I remonstrated with myself for being an idiot, but if I have one thing in my favour in playing golf is that whilst I beat myself up occasionally (and people have commented I'm too hard on myself at times) , mentally it doesn't last too long, and certainly finishes before I play my next shot (usually). As if to prove my point, I went on to the third tee, a par 4 of 313 yards, slammed one down the middle and then played a eight iron to five feet . Particularly pleasing to me was that the flag was nearer the back of the green, and its sometimes difficult to get it all the way up to the hole , but I did. The five footer I faced for birdie was a tricky sidehill putt, but I told myself to play it with confidence, and ram it in for a birdie. Big Mistake. The putt lipped out and finished three foot past. I can imagine you will now be saying "and he missed the one back, didn't he ?" Of course I did, and my second bogey of the day was recorded. Although I don't remember too much about the rest of the round, when I came in and added up my score it added up to eighty blows. With my 74 in the first round a total of one five four was duly recorded as my qualifier scores, and the qualifying mark came at…..one five three. There have been other near misses, but none as painful as that one.

But what of the three successes ? Having qualified three times for the knock out stages, does the name Brian Mooney in gold lettering proudly adorn the Club Championship Board at Milngavie Golf Club ?

Well, the first time I qualified , I was up against Charlie Morley in the last sixteen. Charlie was a decent player, with a handicap three better than mine, so he would definitely have been the bookies favourite. I played well that day however, and Charlie was a bit below par, and although I don't remember too much about the round itself, we shook hands on sixteen as I won 3 & 2. I remember thinking this was good and could indeed be my year. I called David Pirie, my coach and asked if we could meet up on Tuesday to just fine tune my game for the Wednesday. David, somewhat reasonably , given the short notice , said he couldn't fit me in. Unreasonably, I didn't see that as reasonable and (reasonably) decided thereafter that , if I couldn't rely on my coach, I would look after my own game in future. This was probably a bit akin to Tiger Woods dispensing with Butch Harmon's services…..I'm sure he has his good reasons, but was probably a bit hasty and secretly regrets his mistake. Word of advice Tiger – apologise and go back and find your game again. Anyhow, back to the story. My opponent in the quarter final was Kenny Robertson, a very solid player with a handicap five strokes better than me. Again, the bookies would have made Kenny a firm favourite, a kind of 1/5 on to win. I didn't see it that way. I have always reckoned that in anything you do you always have a chance. Liverpool v Wimbledon cup final – just men against men, Mike Tyson v Buster Douglas – just man against man – the underdog always has a chance. If ever I needed confirmation of my excellent chance of winning (although I wasn't counting on this experience), I had crushed Kenny 7&6 in a handicap matchplay game a couple of years earlier, and had we been playing off scratch would have been four up at that point, so I knew it could be done. To cut a long story short, I lost 5&4. My earlier steady play against Charlie disappeared, and Kenny, although not at his best didn't need to be and ran out a comfortable winner. He went on to win the championship that year, and people have said that at least I had the consolation of being beaten by the winner. I must confess I have never found that to be any consolation whatever, but that's just me.

Second time around came three years later, and my opponent was Ian Murray, a good golfer who played off seven. My handicap had drifted up to nine by that time, but I was playing well, and in our game raised that even more, and as we walked down the fifteenth I was three up. The fifteenth at Milngavie is a par 4 of 462 yards and I hit two nice shots into a slight breeze and was twenty five yards short of the green, with a tricky pitch over a bunker guarding the flag. Ian on the other hand had played the hole badly, and his third shot was sliced into rough some thirty yards away. Ian reached his ball first and as I walked up towards my ball he announced he was taking a drop and dropped the ball. I must confess I was taken by surprise. Ian is as honest as the day is long, but I wondered why he was taking a drop. He probably told me but I didn't hear , and I could only assume that there were tyre tracks (where he had landed was in the area where greens staff would drive their equipment on to the course). He played a good shot , twenty feet away in four. I must confess my head was scrambled a bit. Although I'd no cause to doubt him, I'd have liked to have seen the cause of the drop for myself. Truth is, it really shouldn't have mattered in any case. Being three up with four to play, I wisely decided that I would not take the bunker on with a pitch, but instead chip it to the left of the bunker, which would leave me a fifteen to twenty footer for the game, two putts to win if Ian missed his. I took an eight iron for an easy chip and run , and hit it all of…..a foot. Where I should have been concentrating on playing a nice easy shot – bread and butter for me – I can chip and run with the best of them – my head was full of confusion as to why Ian had taken the drop and was he due it, and ….. before I knew it…. I played it ….and…..duff. When I came to my senses, I now had a choice to make. Chip and run fifteen to twenty feet left , or a lob twenty five yards (less a foot now that I had progressed it) over the bunker ? I decided on the latter. Unfortunately I was in no fit state to play the shot and the ball was well and truly bladed, zooming thirty yards through the green at a height of three feet, sending the assembled crowd at the back of the green scrambling. Although my head was as scrambled as the watching crowd had been, I had the presence of mind not to call "Bite, bite!" and thus avoided further embarrassment. A chip on in five and two putts gave me a seven, which, not surprisingly lost to Ian's six.

Nonetheless, I did reckon that I was two up with three to play, so no worries. At the 196 yards par 3 sixteenth, Ian hit his shot just short of the green. I had composed myself enough to slash a five wood way right which was inexorably headed for the out of bounds and into Farmer Pirie's field, when it hit a tree and came back onto the fairway, some thirty yards short of the green. There was no duff chip this time, as I played a nice shot, which somewhat unluckily died a wee bit on the first bounce and came up just six feet short of the hole. Ian chipped up to eight feet and missed the putt, allowing me a six footer to win the match 3&2, just like I did the first time I won in the Club Championship last sixteen just three years earlier. Except I didn't. I hit a nice putt, but just like that putt at Crow Wood some years back, somehow it stayed out. But no matter, I was still two up with two to play.

And then in an incredibly short space of time I was one up with one to play, as I carved my drive out of bounds at seventeen, Farmer Pirie's field finally claiming the ball that was quite clearly destined to find its home there. I hope it's happy wherever it is, plugged deep in the mud or preferably in the middle of one of the copious amounts of coos dung pats that pervades the field.

And so up the eighteenth. Ian hit a good drive up the middle, and given the circumstances, it would have been easy for me to have slashed the ball out of bounds on the right once more. But I am made of sterner stuff than that, and a lunge with my driver produced a topped duff of a shot that even my old dad would have winced at, the ball finishing to rest in the bundai just sixty yards off the tee. I hacked out well, and then hit a seven iron onto the green for three, some twenty five feet from the hole. Ian played a good second some thirty foot away from the flag, and had a putt to square the match.

Well, Ian must've been feeling the pressure just as much as me, because he obviously thought he would lag his putt, just dolly it up there and collect his four, on the justifiable basis that I was in no fit state to hole my twenty five footer. His error. Not that I did hole my putt, but in his efforts to cosy the ball nicely to the hole , he took fright and left it twelve feet short. My twenty five footer came to rest ten inches from the hole for a gimmie, and in for five. Ian now had his twelve footer for a four to square the match. By this time we had a crowd of some twenty people watching us, no doubt wondering how the hell these two hackers had managed to get into the last sixteen of the club's premier competition, the only possibilities being with forged ID or some corruption involving the hitherto unscrupulous officials of Milngavie Golf Club. Whatever they were thinking , there was a hush as Ian faced his putt of destiny. He quite naturally had resolved not to leave this one short, and fairly bashed his putt towards the hole . The ball sped down the green, crashed off the back of the hole, jumped four inches into the air and plonked straight back down again into the cup. Ian exclaimed out loud and punched the air in delight, with a mighty "Yes!". A halved game – and on to the nineteenth to find the winner.

Now it would not be unreasonable to suggest that the tide of the game had turned against me somewhat. At the Ryder Cup the commentators talk about momentum, and mine was most certainly in reverse gear. From being three over par through fourteen to a 7, 4 ,N/R, 5 finish and three up with four to play to being all square, the portents were not good. However, in a strange way, as we walked off the eighteenth green towards the first extra play off hole, I felt strangely calm. It helped that my caddie for the evening, my good friend Dave Allan, is an extremely calm individual. If the Town of Unflappable were looking for an unflappable man to become Mayor Unflappable then Dave would be the man. He's a computer genius for a living, and perhaps talking to computers all day has made him as calm as he is, I know not. What I do know is that at this point he was the ideal companion, not giving me any of the pep talk of "come on we can do this" or "you're the man" or "what a diddy you are for letting a lead like that slip" or any of that nonsense. Anyway, we teed off, and after excellent drives, we both hit two good shots to the first, me being twenty five feet past on the left side, Ian thirty five feet away on the right side of the green. Of the two putts, Ian had by far the most difficult putt. The pin was towards the front left of the green and if he hit his putt a fraction too hard, there was a real danger that the ball would roll off the green and down the slope before coming to rest some thirty yards away. Ian obviously sensed this too, his approach putt coming up twelve feet short again. So here I was, with a putt for the third time to win the match. But I didn't want to take a rush at this one, as Ian was by no means certain of a four, and two putts could be enough. I decided however, not to leave that to chance and to try and hole it. I hit a good putt, but the ball just drifted an agonizing three feet past. Ian's turn. Once again he had obviously decided not to be short and again whacked his twelve footer. I must confess that my first impression was that I wouldn't need to hole my three footer , as with the speed on the ball, and the slope not too far past the hole, his ball would indeed finish some 30 yards off the green. They say that your first impressions are usually right, but not on this occasion as once again, the ball slammed off the back of the hole , jumped four inches into the air and plonked down into the cup. If he was pleased with his putt on the eighteen he was doubly pleased with this one, as once again "Yes!" was heard as the poor battered ball lay resting in the cup. I'm pleased to report that my new found calm that descended on me as I left the eighteenth green was still with me, and I stroked my three footer into the centre of the cup. And so we marched onto the twentieth tee, the par 3 second hole at Milngavie.

Ian, with the honour , struck a beautiful shot which looked all over the flag, but in the fading light we could see it just topple over the back of the green. I hit a decent shot onto the front edge, which left me with a long putt, which I played just about hole high, but breaking six feet left of the cup. Ian , faced with a delicate chip, semi skulled it , the ball running past the flag and by some miracle of nature hung on the lip of the bunker, some 18 feet away. I'm sure I blew hard enough to have it topple over and into the sand, but miraculously it stuck. It was obvious to me that the putter was his next choice, but he persisted with his sand wedge, and instead of semi skulling it, this time he full on thinned it, the ball crashing off the flag and into the hole . For the third hole in succession his pent up emotion was released in a cry of "Yes!". I've often wondered if he recalled those shots he hit in the way I recall them. Maybe I do him an injustice, but I don't think I do. To be fair to all three shots, they were certainly straight…..

If I am to give myself some credit for something, then I suppose I've got a reasonable temperament for these things when they happen, as they do in golf, all the time. They say in all the books you read, "expect the other man to make it, wherever they are." If Tony Jacklin had had the same mentality at Muirfield back in 1972, he, and not Lee Trevino may have prevailed as the Open Champion that year. I must say that even without reading those books, I've always prescribed to that theory. If anyone apologises for a "lucky " shot that goes in, I'll normally respond by saying that there is no need to apologise, you were trying to hole it, weren't you ? So job done, no more to be said. I'm pleased to say that that mentality stayed with me at that moment, and remaining calm , I knocked the six footer in for a half.

The third hole , our twenty first, was halved in par fours, both routine drive, green and two putts, though my second putt was a two footer, which again went calmly in the middle. At this point it was beginning to get really dark, and as the fourth at Milngavie is a long par four up a hill which takes you further away from the clubhouse, someone suggested that we go down the sixteenth, and might just manage the seventeenth if we tied that. Ian, as he had an hour earlier, played a decent shot just short of the green, whilst my well struck shot just edged off the slope at the left side of the green , leaving a delicate shot of some 25 feet, back over the bank that I had just run off. Ian played another decent shot to ten feet, and I, gathering all my experience of playing Cranhill's pitch and putt course, bumped and run a five iron up the hill, on to the green, and coming to rest five feet short of the flag. Ian missed his putt ,and in the darkening gloom, I retained my new found composure and with a smooth putt, holed the slightly left to right breaker right in the middle of the cup. The game was over, and I had progressed into the quarter finals.

As I walked off the course, I must confess I had mixed emotions, which I still have to this day, some 10 years later. I was delighted of course, that I had made it through. But was I a bottler for throwing away a handsome lead down the stretch, or was I made of sterner stuff than most because I had overcome the crisis? I'm not sure I'll ever be able to decide which, maybe a bit of both, but I wish I could bottle up that calm and concentration that I had for the four extra holes. If I could , I'd either sell it for a fortune or win a lot more golf tournaments, that's for certain.

On arriving back at the clubhouse, I learned that my opponent for the quarter finals on the Wednesday would be my club Championship nemesis, Kenny Robertson. If my last sixteen story took a while to relate this one would take a lot less ink. Right from the off I was under the cosh, as my opening tee shot, somewhat unluckily I thought, caught some branches of the last tree on the left of the dog leg. With Kenny bang down the middle , my new caddy for the day, Graham Bell (Dave Allan apparently had been invited to be the Mayor of the town of Unflappable that day) suggested chipping out on to the middle of the fairway and taking my chances from there. No purchase in giving away a hole this early in the round he reasoned. Graham is a solid individual, a school teacher of many years standing , who talks a lot of sense. After considering his sage advice, I waved him away, like Seve would brush any conservative counsel nonsense from his caddy , and demanded a four iron. Like Cameron Watson with his amazing bunker shot, in my mind's eye I could see the shot clearly. I would shut the face, take the club inside on the backswing, roll my hands over at impact, thread it low through the trees, and with a low hook equivalent to Captain Hook's replacement limb it would surely find the green . I would also find Kenny Robertson a gibbering wreck , astounded that he was facing such a genius golfer in the quarter final of a humble Club Championship. Well I did all that, well at least in my head that is. To be fair I did keep it low, so low that it hit a large tree root some four feet from my ball, shot directly upwards ,cascaded off some braches and left me behind another tree with no option but to chip out. This I did, but a shot too late, and Kenny established an early lead, comfortably seeing me off four and three. He won the championship again that year, so at least I was beaten by the winner……

My last and final attempt so far pitted me against Vince Lee, a very steady golfer, and a very nice man, whose handicap was 7 to my 9, so the bookies odds may not have been so generous for this one. After eleven holes, the bookies would have been collecting their cash as Vince was level par, and although I had played decently, I was five over and five down. However, I do remember saying to my new caddie , John Hamilton (both Dave and Graham had given up in disgust) – "I'm not playing badly, this isn't over"….and so it proved. Pars at the next four holes got me back to one down , playing the sixteenth. I bogied the hole however, and Vince parred, so it was two down with two to play. However, having played two great shots to seven feet at the seventeenth, and with Vince in the bunker 30 yards short of the green also in two, all was not lost. He played a good bunker shot to 10 feet and holed the putt, leaving me to hole the seven footer to take it down the last. If I've hit a worse putt in my life, I can't remember it. I was so concerned about the slight left to right break and getting the line right that my putt finished a good 18 inches short. Out by 2&1. Vince , good guy that he is, almost progressed to the final that year, losing at the eighteenth in the semis. Ah well, at least I had the consolation of being beaten by the semi finalist.

As I write this , I'm now starting to appreciate the lure of matchplay that those damned commentators go on about – great fun and varied stories to tell, as distinct from strokeplay which is not as exciting and is more consistent. However, on balance, yup, give me 0.2 off my handicap any time, although I look forward to my experiences from the past Club championships helping me in my future forays to get my name onto the Champions board. If not, I've got some gold leaf paint and stencil at the ready some day when there's nobody about the clubhouse…..

Chapter 16

The Best of the Best

All golfers fancy themselves as golf designers, and I'm no different. I'd love to be given a bit of land to work with and see what kind of course I could craft. I'm a bit of a traditionalist, and some of the American courses I see on the PGA tour makes me shake my head in despair. I'm not a fan of water for water's sake. For example, the 17th hole at Sawgrass with the island green, for me is an abortion of a golf hole. I appreciate it's only 130 yards plus. I appreciate that it causes drama. But no thanks . Too artificial. On the other hand I love it when a golf architect has shaped a golf hole into the natural terrain to complete a masterpiece. Old Tom Morris, James Braid, the Auchterlonies, the Alistair MacKenzie's of the world are the masters. In modern day Kyle Phillips is the man in my view and I also like Dave Thomas. And the great thing about golf is that there are many beautiful sites and views in where the game is played. Yes, I've often thought I'd love to have a go at the challenge of designing my own course. Then I thought – well why not, at least in my head - using holes I'd played before as the basis? Holes and courses that I'd been to and experienced first hand ? Before I go on about my challenge, let me quote a few short excerpts from websites or brochures from some of my favourite courses. Who wouldn't want to play at, or even just be at these places ?

Royal Dornoch

The spectacular panoramic views of the Dornoch Firth and the Sutherland and Ross-shire hills provide the backdrop for Royal Dornoch's location. The curving bay of the Dornoch Firth and its magnificent white broad beaches are backed by a narrow strip of softly contoured dune land rising in two distinctive levels, providing just enough room for parallel fairways. The ridges, hillocks dunes and undulating links land have all the characteristics of the best of links courses……….

Royal County Down

Royal County Down is located in one of the world's most naturally beautiful links settings in the Murlough Nature Reserve.

Against the magnificent backdrop of the Mountains of Mourne, the links stretches along the shores of Dundrum Bay, zigzagging back and forth to provide a different vista from virtually every hole.

The narrowest ribbons of fairways thread their way through as impressive a set of sand dunes as could be imagined. The fairways are sounded by purple heather and golden gorse, so beautiful to look at …..and feature marram, red fescue and heather……

Milngavie Golf Club

Nestled in the awe-inspiring surroundings of Mugdock Country Park, at the starting point for the West Highland Way….this absolutely stunning location provides fantastic views over Glasgow and the central belt as far as the Pentland Hills, and also across to the Campsies and to Ben Lomond……

Turnberry

From the 4th to the 11th, the coastal scenery is magnificent….the 5th to the 8th holes are framed by sandy hillocks, whilst the 9th, 10th and 11th are flanked by craggy rocks. On its stony ridge on the edge of the sea, the 9th hole is Turnberry's trademark. The landmark lighthouse casts shadows over the 13th century ruins of Bruce's Castle, the reputed birthplace of Scotland's hero king Robert the Bruce…..

Even if you don't play golf , wouldn't you want to be at these places ? And if you do play golf, you just have to go.

Anyway, to my challenge. As a renowned , but as yet undiscovered golf course architect, I undertook to put together a course from the many golf courses I have played, with a classic par 72 layout. A challenge in itself, but to add to the difficulty of the task the hole number must be consistent with the hole number of the course in question (i.e. my first hole must be the first hole at course x, my second must be the second at course y , etc). Also in the rules – a course can only appear once, so eighteen different courses must be chosen. This was a difficult part of the quest….some courses are so good they deserve to have more than one hole in a dream eighteen, and some holes which also deserve to be there miss out because I've chosen a hole with the same number from another course. Another aspect to the game is that I can also choose which tee to play from (i.e. it's my call to give each hole Medal or Championship length).

So, for better or worse, here goes …….

Hole 1 Milngavie Golf Club Allander 359 yards Par 4

I like my opening hole on a golf course to be a good par 4, but not a monster (thus counting out the first at Machrihanish, despite my par 4 there!). An almost gentle kind of hole but still having a bit of teeth for the unwary. The first at Milngavie fits the bill perfectly, although if playing it for the first time it may not seem that way, particularly for the higher handicap. First tee nerves are not settled by a mound of whins and heather in the centre of the fairway, which though only some 100 yards from the tee looks a lot further away. For the really nervous , a burn runs across the fairway at a distance of 70 yards of the tee. Trees left and right at landing distance of the tee shot, the fairway dog legs at some 45 degrees left to a raised green, protected by bunkers front left and right. Go too far through the green and rough and more trees await. What was that about a reasonably gentle opening hole ? Well, there's more room on the fairway than you think, and the low handicap golfer would require just a 3 iron to the corner and a nine iron to the green. For an eight handicapper like myself, a good solid drive and an eight iron gets aboard in two. A potential birdie opening, though an easy bogey for the unwary.

Hole 2 Boat of Garten Urie 360 yards Par 4

Again not a long hole and a birdie opportunity for those on their game, and an easy bogey for those not on it. From a raised tee, the silver birches and heather on the right and the heather and the rough on the left are clearly seen . A slight dog leg right, the landing area for the tee shot breaks ever so slightly right to left, and the second shot with just an eight iron has to hold the raised green. Like the first hole, if the pin is at the front you've a difficult choice for the second. Too neat and you don't make it leaving a difficult uphill chip, go too far and the green slopes back to front, leaving a tricky fast downhiller. Not as easy as the card might suggest.

Hole 3 Spey Valley Craig Gourie Par 5

In some ways, another birdie opportunity. A shortish par 5, but to my eye , a nicely shaped hole. From a slightly elevated tee you can see the River Spey flowing all the way down the right hand side of the hole. The drive has to be placed between the bunker on the right at about 230 yards and the bunker on the left at 270 yards. Ideally you want to be down the right hand side as the green is protected by a bunker some 50 yards short left of the green, and a greenside bunker on the right. I'd think that the bigger hitters could fly the first fairway bunker on the right to set up a good birdie chance, but there's enough danger everywhere to make you think.

Hole 4 Royal County Down   229 yards Par 3

Just as you were starting to think that this is a pretty easy start, along comes this beauty of a par 3 . From a tee high up on the hillside there's heather, rough and bunkers just about everywhere, whilst to add to the scenery, the Irish Sea's rugged beauty is to your left and the impressive and imposing Mountains of Mourne form the backdrop directly in front you in the near distance. Wonderful, absolutely wonderful. When I played there I had made par on the first three holes (admittedly at 25mph downwind) and stepped up to this monster which was directly into the wind. I creamed a three wood on to the front of the green, left my 50 foot putt into the wind twelve feet short, and canned the putt for a par. I strode onto the fifth tee thinking I was a golfer. Two and a half hours later, as I signed for my 91, I realised I wasn't.

Hole 5 Turnberry (Ailsa) Fin me Oot 479 yards Par 4

Those "easy" opening three holes must now seem a million miles away. From a slightly elevated tee you can see the green nestling in the hillside on the left some distance away, and all you have to do is drive arrow straight 260 yards to the angle of the dog leg , avoiding the knee high grass and the fairway bunkers both left and right, then hit a perfect 4 iron onto a sloping green, avoiding the three deep greenside bunkers. Take your two putts and leave with a par. I wish I could. I've played Turnberry four times , and despite trying hard to recall such a par, can't say that I can.

Hole 6 Dougalston (Esporta) Lang Drop 207 yards Par 3

The scene of the wildest shot in the history of golf as performed by Frank Geary, the only thing wrong with this hole is its name. You just can't have a mixture of Scottish and English in the name. It's either Lang Drap or Long Drop, make your mind up for God's sake. Lang drop smacks of someone from Milngavie and Bearsden trying to be common in order to fit in with the rabble….starts off with down to earth Scots, then lapses into type and uses the Queen's English. A cracker of a hole, and a three here is cause for celebration. Refer to chapter 5 for full description and details of how not to play the hole !

Hole 7 King's Course Gleneagles Kittle Kink 444yards Par 4

A similar type hole to the 5th in many ways, a long dog leg left but without the elevations . It has a tempting bunker on the left hand side of the fairway. Tempting in that from the tee it looks to the confident golfer that if you drive over that bunker you will shorten the hole considerably. Unfortunately it's a longer carry than you think and there's a bit of rough and heather behind it before you reach the fairway. In four attempts I don't think I ever have , and next time will see me aim right, no doubt catching the heather or the bunker at the right hand side of the fairway. A second shot from the middle of the fairway (or in my case third or fourth, having blasted out of the bunker and/or heather) is still fraught with danger left and right as the rough and heather extend all the way to the green, which is also protected by three greenside bunkers. I'd take a four here anytime, that's for sure.

Hole 8 – Turnberry Kintyre Kintyre's Cove 309 yards Par 4

The signature hole on the Kintyre course with the second shot with a short iron played blind to a green nestling below the level of the fairway and perched just above the craggy rocks and the sea, surrounded by high hillocks of rough wispy golden hay. I say the second is played with a short iron….if the breeze (gale) is directly into your face it will be anything but short ! Two obligatory pot bunkers at the greenside completes the hole. A wee bit of a quirky hole, but worth the inclusion for the scenery alone.

Hole 9 – Muirfield 558 yards Par 5

A good par 5 to finish the first nine. Well placed bunkers down the fairway, with an out of bounds wall running all the way down the left. With the fairway sloping slightly left to right, if you find the bunkers or the rough from the tee, you'll be playing a long third. Should the bigger hitter avoid the bunkers and wants to go for the green in two (breeze permitting) then that out of bounds wall on the left has to be challenged. Scary prospect. There are eight bunkers waiting to catch you out, and like all the bunkers at Muirfield , they are the most magnificent bunkers I've seen, with their sharp, tall, riveted faces. They are indeed things of beauty….unless you happen to be in one of course. Statistics will tell you that this is the easiest hole at the Open in terms of under par scoring. But be warned, statistics can tell you anything and nothing all at the same time.

Hole 10 – Cruden Bay Scaurs 380 yards Par 4

A bit of respite to start the back nine, but like the eighth , a hole worth the inclusion for the views alone. From a very elevated tee, you can see the sea and wonderful landscape all around. Once you've taken your eyes off the scenery, an attractive drive on to a generous and flat landing area below sets up a short iron to the green. But beware. The burn at the front of the green is there to attract those whose attention is taken by the view. A birdie chance ? Yes, but take care, as making sure of getting over the burn and going past the hole will leave you a lightning fast downhiller.

Hole 11 Dundonald 120 yards Par 3

Like the Postage Stamp at Troon (alas I've never played it so it can't be in my selection) proof that a hole doesn't have to be long to be a challenge. Four deep bunkers at the front of the green, the green slopes sharply from back to front, so the temptation is to go an extra club to "make sure" that you're up. Well that would be a mistake, believe me . A ball just over the green will be gathered up, in a golfing vortex, down the slope at the back of the green and into a wicked pot bunker, discarded from Hades by the Devil himself for being too cruel to play from. Should you land in this bunker there are only two possible outcomes. Your first (of many) bunker shots, if not hit hard enough, will come back down the hill to you (and probably into your footmarks). On the other hand, hit it only slightly too hard and you'll be through the green, running with the slope and into one of the bunkers at the front. What about the third option? The shot that's hit just right and stays on the green ? Just like Santa Claus and the Perfect Man, it doesn't exist and is impossible to be played (except for imperious 8 handicappers like myself who splashed out on to the green ,then took two putts and got out of there with a most grateful bogey). A smashing wee hole.

Hole 12 Kingsbarnes   Orrdeal 566 yards Par 5

After the trials and tribulations of the previous hole , being a kindly soul, I give the golfer a bit of a break at the twelfth. Aye , right. A bit of a break at 566 yards, with the sea all the way down the left curving inland to minimise the space for the drive, and the second and the third (and the fourth and fifth in some cases) with penal rough all the way up the right hand side....how can this be termed a break ? Well, in my generosity, I am merely playing this hole off the Medal Tee. Should I have chosen the Championship tee the hole would stretch to a Graeme Jolly taxi fare of twenty quid, a total distance of 606 yards. Those who know me well would be questioning my benevolence...and rightly so. I would've had you playing off the Championship tees except I doubt that I could reach the fairway from there ! (Do I hear faint echoes of "grow some" or "does your husband play golf Mrs.Mooney ?"....but I don't care – Medal tee it is). When you eventually get to the end of the fairway after how many shots , you are then faced with a green in three tiers, a green so large that Scotland play their International Football matches there when Hampden isn't available. Ok, ok , so I made that bit up, but my God, it is huge , and a guaranteed three putts if you're not on the right level!

Hole13 Cawder Keir Course Bearsden 158yards Par 3

A stunningly beautiful par 3. Again, not a long hole, but one in which you can run up a big number. There's a carry to "safety" of some 120 yards, through a lovely avenue of trees . If you're short, long , left or right you're in either rough, rhododendron bushes, trees or a combination of all three. If you're not in there and not on the green or fringe then you're in a bunker. Hit the green ? Well done, but a fast green with subtle borrows ensures no easy two putt, let alone one. Great hole.

Hole 14 Royal Dornoch Foxy 445 yards Par 4

Just a brilliant golf hole, and one of Royal Dornoch's signature holes. At 445 yards, it's quite long, but all "gently" uphill which adds to its length. It has an awkward shaped green, with a bank in front to negotiate before you get on to a tricky putting surface. With no bunkers on the hole and straight up a hill at 445 yards it doesn't sound like a great golf hole, but it is. Play it and see. Definitely not a birdie hole, but a par will seem like one !

Hole 15 East Renfrewshire Slap's Side 376 yards Par 4

The drive goes steeply uphill and at its apex dog legs some 45 degrees left. Don't go too far with the tee shot (not a problem for me) as you risk a downhill lie on to a green some 30 feet below the hill level, protected by a burn at the front, bunkers left and right , and rough and trees at the back. Oh and there's an out of bounds not too far away on the right hand side as well. Get past all of that and there's a possible birdie chance, though with the green sloping back to front, no easy putt.

Hole 16 PGA Gleneagles Lochton Leap 518 yards

Although not my favourite hole at PGA Gleneagles (that honour goes to the fifth which can't make it in due to the rules of the game), this is nonetheless a cracking par 5 of the "risk and reward" category. I've taken the medal tees at 518 yards instead of the championship tees of 543 yards, to tempt the big hitter who has avoided the fairway bunkers left and right to go for it with the second shot over a water carry just 40 yards short of the green. The green itself is well bunkered, and for the shorter hitter or the bigger hitter who has found the rough the lay up place has to be carefully chosen to allow the best approach shot to the flag for the third. Would also make a great men's par 4 off the ladies tee, which gives me the chance to tell you of the 190 yard 5 wood I hit out of the left fairway bunker over the water to twelve feet, when we experimented playing off the ladies tee at that hole the last time we played there. Just thought you'd like to know that. And yes, Mrs.Mooney would not have been able to reach that bunker from the men's tee, thanks for asking.

Hole 17 Old Course St.Andrews Road 455 yards Par 4

One of the most iconic holes in the world of golf , and an automatic choice of hole in my best eighteen. Although probably not necessary to describe, so well known is it, as a recap , conventional wisdom is to either aim left of centre and fade the ball back into the middle off the tee, or fire the ball directly over the wall of the Old Course hotel. From there, avoid the infamous Road hole bunker or shooting too far and on to the road which runs at the back of the long thin green. And that long thin green is raised up three or four feet just to make it more difficult. A truly great hole. But a word of advice for any prospective Open champions needing a 4, 4 finish to win the Open. In my experience, the best way to play the hole is to set up for a gentle fade as noted previously, but instead hit a hook so far left it clears the rough on the left side and runs through the second fairway that runs almost parallel to the seventeenth. From a good lie in the semi , hit a career best 3 wood 215 yards onto the front right of the green and two putt from forty feet for your four. Well that's how I did it…..

Hole 18 Carnoustie Home 444 yards Par 4

Toughest finishing hole in golf ? Probably. Ask Jean Van De Velde who infamously took 7 or even Padraig Harrington, who won in 2007 but took a double bogey 6 there en route to a play off victory against Sergio Garcia. Long, yes. Out of bounds tight all the way up the left. The Barry Burn winding its way up the length of the hole, coming into play several times. Brutal rough on the right hand side, and a bunker to protect the right portion of the green for those thinking of keeping away from the out of bounds when going for the green. Marvellous test. I've not played it in all its glory - I played in winter when the tees were forward and the rough was down, but yes, what a hole to finish. If you needed a four to win and you got it, then you deserve the trophy.

And so there it is. The dream eighteen. Apologies to some courses I've played which were marvellous tests of golf but didn't make the list as I played them so long ago that although I remember them as having great holes (eg Silloth, Dunbar, New Course St.Andrews) I can't remember them clearly enough. Such is old age ! Apologies too to other courses having excellent holes that I did remember (eg Machrihanish, Queens Course Gleneagles, Slalely Hall,) but had to give priority elsewhere, and indeed to other holes on courses chosen (eg second hole at Muirfield, fourth at PGA Gleneagles, fifteenth at Kingsbarnes) that I couldn't include because of the rules. I'm sure they'll all be gutted, but that's life – it's full of tough choices. And being golf, whatever choices you make you can be sure most people will have different opinions on it ! Trust me, I know, I've been on committee .

So, for better or worse, here's the final dream eighteen scorecard. I recommend you having a go at your own during the long winter months, it whiles away a good number of hours !

Hole	Course	Name	Yards	Par
1	Milngavie	Allander	359	4
2	Boat of Garten	Urie	360	4
3	Spey Valley	Craig Gourie	490	5
4	Royal County Down		229	3
5	Turnberry (Ailsa)	Fin Me Oot	479	4
6	Dougalston	Lang Drop	207	3
7	King's Course Gleneagles	Kittle Kink	444	4
8	Turnberry (Kintyre)	Kintyre's Cove	309	4
9	Muirfield		558	5
OUT			3435	36
10	Cruden Bay	Scaurs	380	4
11	Dundonald		120	3
12	Kingsbarnes	Orrdeal	566	5
13	Cawder (Keir)	Bearsden	158	3
14	Royal Dornoch	Foxy	445	4
15	East Renfrewshire	Slap's Side	376	4
16	PGA Gleneagles	Lochton Leap	518	5
17	Old Course St.Andrews	Road	455	4
18	Carnoustie	Home	444	4
IN			3462	36
TOTAL			6897	72

Chapter 17

The Back Nine

At fifty four years of age, you could say that I am approaching the back nine holes of my golfing career. Some may even suggest, somewhat unkindly I hope, that I'm closer to the last two or three. But there's the great thing about golf. Even in the last two or three you can do better than you did before on the previous fifteen or sixteen. And I still harbour ambitions to reach my target of a handicap of five , some forty five years after starting this great game. To those who deal in statistics, this would appear to be unlikely. History would point out that the best I've been is seven and at nearly fifty five my physical (not to mention my mental) wellbeing must surely be in decline. Yet so, I am convinced that I will indeed attain golf's Holy Grail.

The reason ? Well there are a few. What I didn't say in my ramblings about being greens convenor recently was that a year into my stint , Milngavie Golf Club employed the services of a professional for the first time in some twenty five years. David Muir is that man, and a more enthusiastic, positive and encouraging golf pro you could not find. His slogan is "It's all about your game" and he fully lives up to that. Twenty quid for a 30 minute lesson, I've seen him still at the range with me 50 minutes later, determined to see things right. No extra charge. I've yet to meet another pro with that attitude. Thanks to working with him, I've now got my handicap back down to 7.9 as we approach the 2014 season. And that improvement was during my time as convenor! I look forward to more lessons this year to help me attain my goal.

In a bizarre twist of fate, the second reason is down to my brother David. Two years ago, and after some forty years away from the game, David was enticed back onto the course by his brother in law Gerry, who promised "take up the game my son, and you and I will go golfing in Spain and drink lots of beer". It wasn't the fact that he had come back after all that time that has inspired me. It was his approach to it. Determined to rid himself of the wicked slice that bedevilled his game all those years ago, he went to the golf range on a daily basis and practiced and practiced to get rid of that accursed slice. The fact of the matter is that he hasn't , nor has he been to Spain with Gerry yet to drink that beer, and he has now given the game up in frustration, but that matters not. He set out to meet his goal with a steely determination and willingness to put in the time. Here was I , an eight handicap golfer who sometimes plays four times a week in the summer, but who had not attacked golf with such focus since playing on a three times a day basis as a youngster all those years ago. The focus is back. Winter 2013/14 has seen me at the range on a daily basis, in preparation for the golfing season beginning.

And lastly, a changed mental attitude. I've read some of Dr. Bob Rotella's books on the golfing mind, and I wholeheartedly buy into his philosophy – think big, think confidently, and enjoy.

Will all this work ? I am confident that the answer is yes. But what if for some unforeseen reason it doesn't, and Lady Luck farts in my face once more ? What if I don't reach the heights of which I know I am capable ? Well, in the words of the Abba song Waterloo "I feel like I win when I lose"....for I know I'll be playing on a great golf course, supplemented with a few superb away days, playing a sport I love with people whose company I thoroughly enjoy. And that can't be too bad, can it ?

Chapter 18

Hame

In truth, this book nearly closed with the achingly sugary sentimental words at the end of the last chapter. I had related all my stories, it was the start of April 2014, and the golfing season was about to begin, the time when I was going to concentrate all my thoughts and energies into achieving the elusive golfing Holy Grail that is a five handicap. But whilst I was entirely focused on this goal, I realised that there were a few unresolved issues with the book which had to be settled before the publishers could fight over who would be lucky enough to put their name to the next international number one best seller (that would be this book in case you've lost focus). For a start, I had written seventeen chapters but I still had no name for the book. Pretty obviously, eighteen chapters would have been a good number for a golf book, one for each hole in the round as it were, and when I thought about it, "Eighteen" would also be a reasonable title. So what to fill chapter 18 with ? The logical conclusion in my mind was to report on my progression to my destiny of a five handicap. I understood that this would delay the publication of the would be best seller by some six months, or maybe just two months with a burst of early season brilliance. Some cruelly misguided friends advised that an eighteenth chapter on my view of Jack Nicklaus eighteen majors would see the book finished quicker, and would have been more infinitely more interesting, and to them I would say , you're probably right, and thanks for your input , but I'm going to tell my tale anyway……

My thoughts of making 2014 "the year" actually came about just two months previously in November 2013. The golf club AGM had been held at that time, and I had been freed from my prison like tenure as greens convenor. Maria and I were on holiday in Lanzarote and I had taken a Bob Rotella book on the power of the mind with me to read. As I sat in the sun reading his book , Bob spoke personally to me and convinced me that with the right attitude and mental fortitude great things could be achieved. Yes, even a task as gargantuan as attaining a five handicap. And it was there and then that the crusade then commenced.

First things first, a plan. I resolved to hit golf balls every day for 9 months from 1 Jan

2014 to 30 Sept 2014 (the end of golfing season). I would also keep a daily log (recommended by Bob himself) , noting down my good thoughts and the excellent results of my hitting the daily quota of balls. This would reinforce my image of how well I was progressing. I also joined the World of Golf short game area, for within the short game lay the key to success. And I booked 6 lessons with David, the MGC pro. Whilst being totally focused, to ensure I kept to the discipline I revealed my golfing ambitions to a good few people , and thereafter through the winter, told anyone who was interested, and a quite a few who weren't, how well I was playing. Golfers generally, and I am no different, like to keep their light under a bushel, afraid to say they are in good form in case the Golfing Gods overhear them and instantly take it away. I took the view that if I told people (without bragging of course) they would expect me to play well and I'd need to produce the goods. As an added incentive I made a bet with Andy Oxley, our parts manager. As the season approached, I was giving him a hard time over some (for him) poor form. Andy, a blunt Yorkshireman who had attained the legendary five handicap status some years before, had just gone up to six. Not unnaturally, and as golfing friends do, I made maximum capital out of this, and accused him of being a chopper and welcomed him to the ranks of the common or garden hackers . Andy , as he frequently does, took the bait and set off on a rant, demanding an answer as to what handicap I played off. "I am 5.9" he proclaimed, "what are you ?". I avoided the temptation to tell him I was a Sex God. "7.9" came the answer "but the way I'm going and the way you're going I'll be a lower handicap than you come the end of the season". As anticipated, I was then (less than politely it has to be said) asked to put my money where my mouth was. Which I duly did, and a ten pounds wager, or investment as I preferred to call it when he was within earshot, was thus agreed upon. Those who heard about the bet thought I was off my head. "What's the lowest you've been ?" they asked, somewhat incredulously. "Seven point zero" came the response. There then came two further responses from them – firstly that I was mad, and secondly could they get a piece of the action ? On the first charge, no – what they didn't understand was that I still had to reach my full potential, and at some point in the season I was absolutely certain that I would be at 5.4, meaning Andy would have to get his handicap down by at least half a stroke. And secondly, no way am I risking more than a tenner on such a hare brained bet – do you think I am mad ?

Others however, showed more faith in me – well actually they didn't. The aforementioned Bruce Cobburn, now the Thomson McCrone team Captain (handicaps 9 – 20) kept me on the team mailing list , just in case I returned to my nine handicap during the season and his team was struck by the bubonic plague or something and he needed me to play. And the recipient of the wager himself, Andy Oxley, in a fit of sympathy and, despite being the opposition and standing to lose a tenner, did offer some help. In one of the frequent occasions when he would remind me of the enormity and futility of my task, he indicated that he had read a book by Dr. Bob Rotella and he would pass it on in case it would be of use to me, because I would surely need some kind of help or at least a minor miracle. He then asked our respective handicaps once more and concluded "no chance". This struck me as strange as Dr.Bob's book was all about confidence as a means to improvement…..had Andy actually read and understood any of it ? I indicated that there was no need as I had read it and politely declined his offer, in a language he could understand. "No thanks you Wazzock, geet that tenner out tha's breeches and be ready t' hand't ower at end t'season".

So how did the season start ? Well not too good I'm afraid to say. First four medals of the season ? Played reasonably well but missed the buffer zone by one each time for the first two, made the buffer in the next and missed by about a million in the fourth and went up by 0.3 to 8.2, all by the end of April. It was little consolation that Andy had gone up 0.4 to 6.3, so I had closed the gap. Chipping and pitching was still a problem, my game had gone slightly off the boil , and my putting was erratic (early season greens obviously), but a couple of lessons from David gave me renewed hope. The first signs that all would be well came in a foursomes match early in May. For fourteen holes all four of us played some of the worst golf that any of us could remember, but in the midst of this I played four excellent pitches over bunkers at 6, 15, 16 and 17 when the pressure was on. That showed me I was on the right track. A putting lesson the next day from David firmed up my putting stroke, and so I faced the month of May with renewed confidence. As the ground started to dry up with some better weather, a few practice rounds suggested I was coming back to my best form.

As you probably appreciate, when the ground starts to dry up in the West of Scotland due to the better weather, it's not long until a deluge comes along to restore the natural quagmire conditions that makes golf such a delight in these parts. And so it proved on the morning of the first qualifier of the Club Championship on the 7th May. After an inspection and clearing several greens of water, the head greenkeeper proclaimed the course "just about open". After discussions with my playing partners it was decided that we would play, give it 7 holes and see what it was like at that point. I confess as to not being entirely convinced – if we stopped after 7 holes my handicap would go up 0.1 and despite wanting to play in the club championship the priority was to get my handicap down. Given the uncertainty, I didn't enter the competition, but went out with the guys to play as many holes as the weather permitted. Of course , after 4 holes the weather brightened, and I lost the chance to post a score for the club championship and the chance to get my handicap down.

I had appreciated however that all was not lost with regards to meeting my target, or indeed to the championship, as the qualifying for this is the best two of four scores, so I still had the next three weeks to qualify. After the first two of these I had shot 78 and 76 – not good enough to get my handicap cut, but not up either, and I lay in 13th place out of the 16 qualifiers with one more qualifier to play. Now I'm not proud – when it comes to club championship qualifying I'll take it by any means necessary . Bubonic plaque strikes Milngavie and surrounding district and takes out its eight best players ? What a pity, but as long as I'm in the top 16, I don't care. I was thus hoping for a major league storm come the final qualifying day, or at least a mini tornado, to prevent anyone out of the top 16 interloping in and usurping my quest to win the championship even before the knock out stage had begun. It was thus disappointing to read the weather forecast during the week to see that Saturday was to be a balmy eighteen degrees celsius with clear skies and….. worse than that , almost wind free. Damn ! Perfect golfing conditions – in the West of Scotland - what was all that about ? What an injustice ! After much soul searching I persuaded myself that this was a good thing. It would force me to improve my score and at the same time get my handicap cut to move towards my ultimate goal. My mindset had changed immediately to - excellent – bring it on !

Now people say that you should not interfere with things that are going well. If it ain't broke then don't fix it. I had achieved a decent score in the first two rounds and was playing good golf. I had forged an excellent mindset, which by all accounts is at least half the battle. But I still wasn't entirely happy. Whilst the majority of the golf was indeed good, there were four or five ropey shots a round in there and I reckoned that with a bit of tightening up I could be almost guaranteed to make inroads into my handicap and also secure my place in the club championship matchplay stages. So a lesson was organised with David and we agreed on a shortening of the backswing (it had started to make John Daly's swing look like a truncated hockey swing) and hitting more against a firm left side. That phrase "hitting against a firm left side" had bugged me for years. What exactly did that mean ? David explained exactly that by showing me a video of my swing , which although flowing, had me bending my left knee outwards near impact like an English longbow and thus losing my height. A "firm left side" involved a bit more rotation with the hips to keep the left side from moving towards the target. Technical stuff over, though if you wish to make a donation having helped your golfing knowledge, that'll be twenty quid, just send it to my account.

Even as I practiced this move, at this stage in the season I was also conscious about the final outcome of the book. Would it be a triumph for hard work and diligence or would the glass ceiling of a handicap of 5.5 (or indeed my previous best of 7.0) remain, and forever never to be broken? To those now thinking that it would still be possible to achieve it in years to come, I had undoubtedly put that scenario out of reach by accepting an approach by Derek Hunter, this year's Vice Captain at MGC, to take on his role in 2015 and thus become Captain in 2016 . In 2017, as Past Captain I would still be on the committee. Improvement in those years would be , as had been evidenced in times gone by, completely impossible. It was alleged that Tom Cruise as agent Ethan Hunt in Mission Impossible had refused to attempt such a task as being too difficult. At the end of this period I would be nearly sixty years of age and so 2014 had to be the time. Could I do it, or would it be a hard luck story, or indeed a not even close story ? I must confess, despite Dr.Bob's inspiring words to me some six months earlier, and my excellent mindset I was beginning to have my doubts. Not that I told anyone that of course....I was still working through my plan after all, the results just hadn't entirely kicked in yet.

In a strange way, my resolve was boosted by the fact I reckoned that I wasn't just doing this for myself any more. My coach and friend David Muir had invested much time , belief, and in some respects, his own credibility in the project. (Sooo David, Brian was telling me you've given him copious hours of lessons and coaching and his handicap went up from 7.9 to 9.7 ? Interesting. Interesting. Sounds.... gooood. Tell you what, I'll come back to you regarding that lesson I was going to book…..). So it would be great if I could achieve it , not just for myself, but for him too.

It would also have been great to see the name Brian Mooney on the Club Championship board in 2014, but sad to say it became evident that maybe, apparently , this was not to be. The weather on the last Saturday qualifying was indeed perfect and there was a raft of low scores, but alas none of these were mine, and my total of 154 missed out by two shots as I crashed down the field to 19th place. My miserable last round of 85 was the season's poorest to date.

So what went wrong that day? Well, I had reached the turn in 40, having missed three shortish putts which could have got me out in 37 and a decent front nine. However even at that, back in 36 was eminently do able and as I stood on the tenth tee I had gone into my mantra of one shot at a time and see where that got me at the end of the day. I was determined not to get carried away if I started to reel off par after par interspersed with the occasional birdie on the back nine. Well, there wasn't much danger of that as my well struck tee shot at the tenth just failed to clear the rough cladden hill some 150 yards off the tee and bounced backwards into an almost impossible lie in the bundai. It was in the midst of this crisis that my newly found excellent mindset kicked in. I reasoned that a hack of 40 yards with a wedge would get me back onto the fairway and within distance of the green, where a well struck 3 wood would find the target , leaving a putt for par. That well constructed plan soon disintegrated as my initial hack went one fortieth of the distance required, travelling a distance of all of a yard. More hacks, a duffed chip and three putts from three feet saw me complete the hole in eight, and the dream was over for another year as I limped home in 45.

Championship hopes over, two things were evident to me as I played in the Tuesday medal the following week and shot 81 to see my handicap rise to 8.4. The first thing was that whilst I had shortened my backswing and was convinced that this was the right way to go, my timing wasn't great with it , and I had a choice – go back to the John Dalyesque swing to get my rhythm back, or persevere with the shorter (better) backswing and hope it would come good sooner rather than later. For me this was a no brainer, and I arranged another lesson with David for the following Sunday to ensure I was sticking to the correct backswing and for some words of wisdom on timing. The second thing that was evident to me was also a no brainer. The putter had to go. Many will be astounded at that statement. What had happened to the putter that had won Phil Mickelson the Masters, the putter that whilst maybe was not quite up to the legend of my original hickory wand , was still going to be good enough to sweep me to my target ? Those who play golf will know that golf, and putters in particular, can be cruel mistresses. Like a young seductress, who excites and promises in equal measures early in your relationship, then as time goes on and you get married, transforms before your eyes into the bitch from hell who ruins your life forever. Obviously I have had no experience of the latter, I'm just using this as an analogy based on what others have told me, but the point is the putter had to go. David had spotted I was breaking my wrists at impact when putting, but in my view this detail was largely irrelevant as I had concluded that the demon that had now possessed the putter was permanently ensconced and that even an excellent putting stroke was doomed to failure using the tarnished and infected implement. I had considered getting the local parish priest to conduct an exorcism, but instead chose to consign the offending Odyssey number nine putter to the naughty corner of the upstairs cupboard , to join the six other putters who had committed similar serious felonies over the years. Its place in the bag was taken by another Odyssey putter, just like the one that Luke Donald, the finest putter on tour uses. Having holed several putts on the golf shop's indoor practice mat (just a thought - do these mats all slope in towards the hole to ensure success ?), I was sure that I was back on track. This feeling was bolstered somewhat after the Sunday lesson with David who confirmed that whilst I now had shortened my backswing to a perfect parallel, my set up had gotten a bit upright and I had fashioned a bit of a reverse pivot, one of my (previously) common faults, hence not striking the ball with the authority that one would associate with a five handicap. A few wise words from my mentor, and twenty minutes later I was hitting the ball better than I ever had before, and I couldn't wait to get out in the next medal.

And then a strange thing happened. On the Monday I received an email from Match and Handicap asking if was I available for the last 16 knockout stages of the Club Championship. Fairly obviously , three of the guys who had qualified in front of me couldn't make it , and thus I was in. Rumour had it that the first guy was seriously injured in a car crash after his brakes failed, the second one had his home petrol bombed in apparently a random attack from the previously unheard of Milngavie Freedom Fighters and the third had mysteriously vanished without a trace and was not able to be contacted. I cannot comment on these rumours, at least not until the police have completed their search in the woodlands and concluded their investigations, which I had hoped would extend at least until the Club Championship had passed. Whatever the reasons, I was in, and as sixteenth qualifier I was drawn to play the Club Champion of last year and two times winner, Alan Foggo, who it was said, had withdrawn to a "safe house" just in case .

Although I was delighted to be involved at the knock out stage and I had no real fears of playing Alan (handicap just 6 strokes better than me) as the week progressed I was a wee bit concerned that the changes that David and I had worked on weren't working 100% of the time. I had by now drifted up to 8.5, but I reckoned that destiny awaited. Like the Denmark football team of 1992, who only got into the Euro Championships at the last minute following troubles in the Balkans and won it despite being complete underdogs, my time had come. To ensure this, I now sought the services of a caddie. If all this sounds a bit serious to the reader, just let me assure you that having a caddie in these big events is a very good thing indeed. A second opinion on a club selection or a read at a line of a putt can make the difference between winning and losing. Just having your man on the bag makes you feel like a golfer, gives you confidence. Speaking of which, my friends John Hamilton and Andy Murrison who had both promised to caddy for me if I made it to the last 16, had so much confidence in me that they booked up holidays for the knock out stages. Cheers lads, thanks for that. I had also asked that Unflappable man, Dave Allan, if he was available, but alas he was going to be writing a major software programme that would create instant World Peace or prevent a world banking crisis or something that very weekend. No sense of priorities that man. Unflappable yes, sense of priorities, no. Junior convenor James Williams was also asked, but it transpired that he was looking for payment and the idea was quickly shelved. In desperation I called Bruce Cobburn, that man of infinite golfing wisdom, and captain of the Thomson McCrone team, and the conversation went thus:

"Hello Bruce, it's Brian Mooney here. (I then hear some noises in the background). You don't sound as if you're at home. Where are you ?"

"I'm at the Dental Hospital"

"Oh, sorry to hear that, what happened ?"

"I stubbed my toe".

I hesitated, wondering should I be asking this idiot to be my caddie or not, but I was desperate to look the part on the day, so the question was asked, and he agreed. And sure enough, next day he arrived, right on time, munching on a sandwich as such was his devotion to the cause that he was just coming off the course having played it earlier that morning and had noted the all the pin positions. Alan, as defending Club Champion had no need for such showmanship as he arrived alone, deciding no doubt in his mind that no extra help was necessary. And to cut a long story short, he was right. Pars were collected to the Foggo account with alarming ease, and whilst I collected a fair few myself, it was not enough. I had drafted my Odyssey number nine putter back out of the naughty cupboard (the new baby proving to be a bit more unreliable than it was in the golf shop) and whilst I hit a number of good putts, there were a few crucial near things from close to mid range that didn't fall, which might have made the match a bit closer than the 5&4 drubbing that followed. To be fair, despite the defeat the game was hugely enjoyable and Bruce the bagman was an invaluable source of encouragement, noting as I went one down after three "never mind Brian, you'll be getting a stroke at the fourth…..oh that's right it's a scratch competition….you don't get strokes", and laughing uproariously at my uber positive suggestion of "get ready to go up the nineteenth Bruce" as I went up the fourteenth hole five down with five to play.

Club Championship out of the way (Alan got to the final by the way, so at least I went out to a finalist….still no consolation) I could now concentrate fully on my real goal. I was encouraged by the way I hit the ball on that day and was convinced that I was not far away from where I needed to be . A slight shortening of the backswing on the irons, a more stable putting base and maintaining my height by not dropping my hips whilst chipping and pitching and my game would be in excellent order for the remaining three months of the season.

But before revealing the last stage of the chapter and the conclusion of whether I made it or not, just let me relate a wee story which occurred in the final of the MGC club championship which to me illustrates the beauty of golf. As indicated, Alan Foggo had reached the final and as defending champion, was in good form. Apart from dispatching me 5&4 , he had seen off his quarter and semi final opponents 3&2 and 6&5 respectively. So it must've been a bit of a shock to him then to find himself seven down with eleven holes to play to his young opponent in the final,Steven Cafferty. Steven had only just joined Milngavie earlier in the season, and has an exceptionally fine swing. As a by the by he is also registered deaf and we'd held a day on his behalf to help send him to the World Deaf Golf Championships in the U.S.A.. He works at World of Golf in Drumchapel, where some members of staff there have unkindly suggested he's only deaf when he's being asked to do something he doesn't particularly want to do, but that's yet another story which I'm unable to comment on. What I do know is that he was playing fantastic golf in the final, which I had turned up to watch (to see how it should be done) , so it was some surprise that his well struck iron off the tee at the 26th hole drew a bit more than he had anticipated, and found heavy rough some 120 yards away from the pin. Alan meantime, sensing a glimmer of hope, creamed one straight down the middle, leaving a shot of some 100 yards. Looking at his lie, I had some doubts as to whether Steven could reach the green, but with a majestic swish he sent the ball out of the rough. Now although we couldn't see the ball land as it made its way over the hill just short of the green , it had started a touch left but then kicked right and we knew it wouldn't be far away. Undaunted, Alan hit his approach over the hill, right down the stick and as we walked over the brow of the hill there was just one ball on the green , lying nicely some five foot short of the flag. Steven was first on to the green and he looked at the ball, and realising it wasn't his, then looked into the cup. He looked round to Alan, shrugged his shoulders , hands upturned apologetically, bent down to pick his ball out of the cup , but when halfway down straightened up and said " Na – I'm only kidding". His ball had actually gone just through the back of the green – just out of sight of Alan and the rest of the crowd who were standing at the front end of the green ! Alan's face was a picture – but it is to his eternal credit he burst out laughing as did everyone else. Brilliant.

Steven then just missed with his chip and Alan had recovered sufficiently to hole his putt for a birdie to win the hole, but it was just a magic moment of humour and sportsmanship . Alas for Alan, there weren't any other chinks of light for the remaining holes as they matched par with par and Steven saw out the match 6&5. Full marks to both guys.

I returned to work on Monday, inspired by the weekend's events and more determined than ever to reach my goal in the coming three months. But as I opened my emails that morning there was a blow for me and European golf in general with the contents of an email from Andy Oxley, the Yorkshireman who had been so foolish to have made the £10 bet with me. He had copied me in with a notice from howdidido , a site which registers handicaps, proudly announcing he was the recipient of a handicap change to....5.2 . He had shot a gross 69, and had come down a full 1.4 in one go. After I retained my composure, I called him to say that far from being disheartened, I had been boosted in the knowledge that if he could do it, well anyone could do it . (Except I'd need to do it three times, but needless to say I didn't go into that level of detail, although equally needless to say, he did).

It would be fair to say that the confidence I had at the start of the season had diminished somewhat, but I still had hope. Looking through my scores of previous seasons on howdidido , I realised that most of my good scores occurred in July and August, and this was confirmed somewhat on the 1st of July when I shot a nice 76 in the Seniors Championship Qualifying round. It was then that irony, or karma, or serves you right or whatever you want to call it came into play. On reaching the age of fifty five I was in my rookie season in the seniors at MGC. I reckoned that I was I dead cert to qualify for the last eight of the Championship knockout stages. My logic was undeniable. Although there were a good number of very tidy golfers among the seniors, the odds, I reasoned , were heavily in my favour. Of the sixty or so people eligible to play, I reckoned that fifty percent had a handicap of over eighteen. As this was a scratch competition, by laws of averages, this would surely eliminate them. I also reckoned that at that age of the seniors some twenty percent would simply forget to turn up, and another twenty percent would either die off or have some serious illness which would prevent them playing. This would leave me a guaranteed top six place. So where did the karma come in ? Well, two days after my fine 76, I was at work in the office, stood up from my seat and promptly collapsed. Some fifteen minutes later I was brought round and taken to Wishaw General Hospital where after some heart tests it was concluded that I probably had a viral infection. Some blood tests later showed no long lasting problems but the viral infection had "taken me out the game" so to speak. A very light headed feeling allied to the strong desire to go to sleep every hour put an abrupt halt to any golfing activities. An abrupt halt except that I had indeed qualified for the last eight of the Seniors Championship and I had been drawn against my good friend Euan McGregor to be played just two weeks later. Perhaps stupidly, I was determined not to be one of the twenty percent who missed out due to death or illness, and I turned up for the quarter final, feeling somewhat less than one hundred percent. As I teed it up on the first and some black dots obscured my vision, I decided that if I was three down after seven (where we would be back close to the clubhouse) I'd concede the tie and get back home safe.

There is a saying in golf "beware the injured golfer" and as I reached the seventh green two up this was proving to be the case. Much to my surprise I continued to play well, but Euan covered the next nine holes in level par, finishing me off with a birdie two at the sixteenth for a three and two victory. He went on to to win his semi final before being narrowly beaten two and one by defending champion Iain Gardner in a high quality final. Oh well, at least I had the consolation of being beaten by a finalist.

There was also the crumb of comfort that I had indeed arrived as a senior golfer proper. When younger, the chat on the course and at the 19th among the guys would be about golf, football and women. I quickly learned that as a senior this changes to what illnesses you have had and who has died since last week. Well, with my collapse at work I was sure to fit in, as I could wax lyrical about my mysterious and debilitating illness. I soon learned however that in this regard I was strictly second division. Tales of acute arthritis, hip replacements, shingles and pancreatic cancer rendered my feeble blip almost worthless. But at least I had made a start. And I also learned a valuable lesson. When describing illnesses to friends at senior level, you must give it the gravity it deserves. Hence my faint at work became a blackout and latterly a collapse…..

That said, feeble illness or not, the months of July and August were not particularly kind to me. I would think I was making a recovery, play a few holes of golf, but the viral infection would kick in and I'd suffer for it the next few days. I thus was reduced to chipping and putting for an hour on Saturday afternoons, rather than shooting the lights out in medals. Andy Murrison and I were however , still in the fourball knockout and I played in the quarter final and then semi final feeling less than great but fortunately able to win through to the final. Still no medal rounds played, and my handicap remained at 8.8. Meantime, my deadly rival Andy Oxley had further reduced his handicap to 4.9, and thus my tenner seemed sure to find it's way over the border, not that that bothered me too much – I just wanted to get back playing ! By the time mid September came Andy had gone up to 5.2, so all was not lost – all I needed was a course record scratch 59 in the final medal of the year to win !

Before that however, was the matter of the final of the fourball, and we played this on the 21st September on what was a beautiful day for golf. I hadn't been on a course for some five weeks but played decently, and fortunately my partner Andy was in excellent form. Unfortunately, despite his excellence, we were beaten at the last hole by the sparkling golf of the father/son combination of Phil and Chris Low, who it was rumoured had a direct lineage to Jesse James or some other cowboy bandit. One might have been bad enough, but with both being of the same bandit blood line what chance did we have ? Ah well, at least we were beaten by the winners. Despite the result, I thoroughly enjoyed the game and the boys company, and realised I was getting soft in my old age.

So to the final medal of the year. Did I go out on a high and if not attain my goal , at least exit the season in a blaze of glory ? Na. In short, I gave in to the viral infection again and didn't play. I'm sure I could hear Andy Oxley breathing a sigh of relief all the way from Yorkshire.

So there we have it. Forty five years of golf. Another season of toil, anguish, frustration and more than a bit of fun, but ultimately a failure to reach my goal. But is it really over for my golfing ambitions ? I was heartened by the knowledge that many an achievement has been made by the maxim of "if at first you don't succeed, lower your standards". So should I target a return to eight handicap for next year and make that the goal for success? Na – not in my nature. But alas I have to accept the fact that Lady Luck has indeed properly farted in my face and now as I go to join the committee for the next three years, I'm resigned to the realisation that my lifelong ambition of a five handicap will never be attained. Acht well, in the words of the Abba song Waterloo "I feel like I win when I lose"….for I know I'll be playing on a great golf course, supplemented with a few superb away days, playing a sport I love with people whose company I thoroughly enjoy. And that can't be too bad, can it ?

Bollocks.

2015 is the year . With all the work I put in and the improvements I made in 2014 ? Five handicap beckons for sure. Where's Oxley's phone number so that I get that bet on ?

19th Hole

There are various topics of conversation after a round at the bar or the 19th hole. As I've indicated, these range from football, golf and women for the guys to illness and death for the older members, but I don't wish to discuss any of these here. As this could be my one and only book that I ever write, I'd just like to share these random thoughts. Make of them what you will….

Jesus said "I am the way, the truth and the life". Having heard and read what he did and said, I'd buy that.

I know it's sad, and I'm not sure I can explain it, but one of my great pleasures in life is coming out of a petrol station having a full tank of petrol.

I'm not an advocate of the Hare Krishna movement, but Gouranga, be happy. Can't argue with that.

No matter what I do for the rest of my days, my greatest two achievements in life will be my son Paul and daughter Stacey. And my wife Maria had more to do with my greatest achievements than I did !

I secretly admire the persistence and patience of Jehova's Witnesses.

I have various ordinary grades, higher grades, an honours degree, a professional accountancy qualification, yet a five year old can work a mobile phone better than I can.

Family and friends. Can't get better than that.

And lastly, the viral infection that played havoc with my golfing year has made me realise that the goal of the five handicap wasn't as important as I thought it was. Not that I'll ever stop trying however. I am, first and foremost , a golfer after all….

Made in the USA
Charleston, SC
12 December 2014